TWO WHEELCHAIRS
AND A
FAMILY
OF THREE

TWO WHEELCHAIRS
AND A
FAMILY
OF THREE

Fred V. Camp

TYNDALE HOUSE PUBLISHERS
Wheaton, Illinois

Coverdale House Publishers Ltd.
London, England

Library of Congress Catalog Card Number 72-96214
ISBN 8423-7650-X

Copyright © 1973 by Tyndale House Publishers,
Wheaton, Illinois 60187

First printing, February, 1973
Printed in the United States of America

Dedication

To Bea . . .

> my inspiration and help in writing
> this book,
> and my true helpmate
> through our years together;

and to Julie . . .

> who has been all that a daughter could be
> to her father and mother.

Contents

Foreword

Two Wheelchairs and a Family of Three was written for the sole purpose of giving a helping hand to the thousands of handicapped people in the world, and helping physically able persons to understand the needs of the handicapped. I've tried to keep this aim always before me as I have related my problems and experiences.

Life has brought me some good times — some perplexing times — some bad times — but each situation has had to be met and dealt with. Forty years of living in a wheelchair and making one's own way financially and socially can be uplifting — or discouraging. As I have met each situation in life, I have tried to be ready to offer help and understanding to other handicapped persons.

It has been my experience that though he may not realize or admit it, almost everyone in the world is somewhat handicapped — physically, mentally, socially, or spiritually. If through reading this book you gain insight into the victory available to all, it will not have been written in vain.

Fred V. Camp

Salem, Oregon
January, 1973

1

The End

"Hey, Mr. Jensen, let her come!" I shouted up to the farmer whose well I was helping dig. And little did I know that those six words would signal the end of one life for me and the beginning of another.

I was eighteen and had always lived around Kenmare, North Dakota, so farm work was nothing new to me. I was helping Mr. Jensen because I was a laboring man and there was work to be done — work that kept me strong and in good physical shape for my favorite sport of boxing. I had only a little more excavating to do, but the debris had to be hauled out before the curbing could be lowered. I worked at top speed through the afternoon because I had a date with one of the most popular girls in our community that night and

I had to get ready. I had made all the arrangements and my spirits were high. All I could think about was the fun we'd have with our friends that night.

I got the excavating done and all the dirt crumblings neatly carved out and was ready for the curbing to line the well. The winch and shaft were poised over my head and the curbing swung there above me.

"Hey, Mr. Jensen," I called. "Let her come."

And come it did! It all came — the curbing, the winch, the shaft — all at one time, and it landed right on top of me. I had never had anything hit me like that in all the fights I'd had boxing. I was literally floored! I couldn't get up. I couldn't move. I tried, oh, how I tried; but I just couldn't move.

I must have screamed for Mr. Jensen to get me out. The water was seeping in and the last thing I wanted was a watery grave. He leaned down and groped for me, but he soon saw he could not get me out by himself. He had to get help. Trouble was, we were in a part of the North Dakota farming community where a man and his wife and his hired help made up the entire population for miles around and Mr. Jensen's wife had given birth to a son that very morning. She couldn't help and he didn't want to get her excited and upset when there was nothing she could do.

He would have to run across the fields to get a man at a neighboring farm to come help him, but he didn't want to leave me alone. He did have a hired girl helping his wife, however, so he ran to the house to summon Bernice before going for the neighbor.

For me, every minute I stayed down in that well was an eternity. The water kept seeping in, and soon I was covered by several inches; by the time he returned, I was half covered. First, they threw me a rope; but, try as I would, I could not tie that rope around myself. Finally, the neighbor had to be lowered into the well to secure the rope around me so they could pull me out.

I remember today, after forty years, how extreme the pain was as they lifted my 170 pounds, inching me upward until finally they pulled me over the side. There I was in agony, soaking wet and muddy, with no doctor anywhere to alleviate my suffering. The two men and Bernice carried me to the house. I can still see Bernice standing in the doorway, a frightened look on her face, wondering not only what would happen to me next but how seriously I was hurt. There was no way of getting an ambulance and the nearest hospital and doctor were seventy miles away.

I can't really remember the next hours too well — only incidents that occurred in them. I remember Mr. Jensen's trying to get his tudor car fixed so I could lie on the floor. I just could not sit up. He did remove one of the seats, but even then it was not a very desirable ambulance. I remember his asking me how to contact my father. He called Dad and arranged to stop by our home in Kenmare to pick him up, since that was right on the route to Minot's Trinity Hospital. I remember telling Mr. Jensen to call ahead for a Dr. A. R. Sorensen so that he would be available. My sister Enger, a registered nurse, had graduated from Trinity, and the name of Dr. Sorensen was one I had often heard. I knew she still had great admiration for his work and ability, even though she was far away in Portland, Oregon, working as Supervisor of Nurses at Emanuel Hospital. I remember stopping to get my father and I remember the look of anxious concern on his face.

Next, I remember arriving at Trinity and finding Dr. Sorensen waiting for me. After a series of X-rays and several consultations, the doctor informed my father that a laminectomy, an operation on the back, must be performed in order to help me.

My father came into my room, so quiet and so concerned, and said, "Fred, you have some chance if the doctors operate, but you must decide."

Operate? Of course. Let's go. How could an 18-year-old say anything else? I had plans — great plans — about what I was going to do with my life. Of course we'd operate.

I can still remember the surgery. The doctor was skeptical about giving me an anesthetic because of the possibility of pneumonia. I faded in and out of consciousness, but I felt no pain. I remember the doctors and nurses talking and working. I can remember seeing pieces of fractured bone that they removed from my back. And I can remember being taken back to my bed after surgery.

I look back on Trinity Hospital now with fond memories, as it seemed to me I was almost considered a special guest there rather than a patient. Mother and Dad called my sisters who lived in Portland, and they immediately came home. Enger, leaving her job at Emanuel, became my special nurse and my sisters Lydia and Ella assisted in my care. Enger stayed with me each day as long as I needed her and then she worked with other patients. I was given my choice of available student nurses for the remainder of my stay at Trinity and I especially remember Neva Hought, who did a marvelous job for me. She later was graduated from Trinity and is now at a hospital in Eugene, Oregon.

Newspapers brought into my room would frequently have a clipping cut out — even current papers. Finally I came to realize that these articles were about me and that the nurses didn't want me to read them.

I had more company than any hospital would allow today. I had been active in our school and church groups and community gatherings, so company came by the carload. We kept a register which showed that 350 guests entered my room in the seven weeks I was at Trinity. Those people! I can never thank them enough for all the help they gave me and for their encouragement.

But one guest, a neighbor from Kenmare, came into my room one day, walked up to my bed, looked at me as if I were already dead, and said calmly, "Too bad you'll never walk again."

Never walk again? Never *walk* again? Too bad I'll never walk again? Suddenly all the pieces fit together. My father's sober, almost tearful, concern when he told me the doctors would have to operate. He must already have been told that I would not walk again. And the neat holes in the newspapers — the items that had been cut out must have told about the hopelessness of my case, and that was why so many people had been coming. That was why my sisters had come and stayed and helped me. And that was why everyone was being so nice to me at the hospital.

It all fit together, thanks to this neighbor who never visited me again. It all fit together — and I was crushed. I had been so consumed with the thought of getting well. I had felt that all I needed was time and my legs would function as usual. I was so sure we had won the chance the doctors had given me when they operated.

They got the "neighbor" right out of my room, but the words could not be unsaid, and the damage was done.

I saw it all now. He was right. I would never walk again.

2

A New Beginning

After seven weeks in Trinity Hospital, I was going home to Kenmare — back to the only place I had ever lived. The railroad company did not have any facilities to take a stretcher patient, so it arranged to put an extra baggage car on a passenger train. Imagine! A baggage car for me who in those weeks had dropped in weight from 170 pounds to 100 pounds — just skin and bones.

Those sixty miles were the longest I have ever traveled, for it seemed that we stopped at every station. We finally pulled into Kenmare for what I had thought would be a very quiet homecoming. But to my great surprise I saw the whole platform crowded with people who had come to welcome me — home! They had not expected to see me ever come home again, but here I was.

Kenmare had no ambulance in 1929; it didn't even have a taxi cab. But I was provided with one of the very best conveyances, because my friend Bill Peterson was on hand with his coal truck — the biggest in all that country. And he drove me home in that as if it were loaded with goldfinch eggs.

As we drove along, I reveled in all the old familiar landmarks — even to the ruts in the old gravel road that I had helped fill and the broken-down fence that I should have replaced or repaired.

And now in a few minutes I would see Rover. How I had missed seeing my dog. I wondered if he would remember me. I thought of the times we had gone hunting together — my horse Pat, the dog and I. I thought of the coyotes we had chased, the minks we had trapped, the rabbits we had bagged. What a dog! I thought of the foggy days when we could not see where the cattle had gone and of how old Rover had brought them home by himself, so careful to get them all and not hurry them on the way. I thought of the bulls he had helped me part after a terrific fight which destroyed at least an acre of our grain.

So when we got home, my first question was,

"Where's Rover?" I was sure he would have come running out to greet me.

"Fred," Mother said hesitantly, "Rover's not — well, he's not with us any more."

"What?" I was incredulous.

"He was killed just yesterday. Our neighbor ran over him with his car. Somehow he'd gotten under the wheels and . . ."

I was crushed. My whole homecoming was suddenly — just not so important after all.

So here I was back home — and now what? I thought of the lake beside our home — a beautiful lake twenty-five miles long and a mile wide. Would I ever swim or skate there again? When the lake froze over in winter we had wonderful skating. There wasn't a boy in the whole community that couldn't skate. On a Sunday afternoon there would be at least twenty-five of us on that ice. Usually a group of kids from five miles north of us would skate down to our place or all of our group would skate to theirs. Then we would put our sleds or toboggans behind a team of horses on the lake and grab on to a long rope for some lightning fast crack-the-whip.

One day I had tried to be smart and jump on a moving toboggan; but just as it went by, it caught my heels and turned me right over in the air. People laugh about that to this day.

That ice, though, had nearly been the death

of four of us one time. We had skated down the lake about four or five miles, looking for spots on the lake where the ice was really smooth. It was so much more fun to skate on glass than on frozen ripples. On our way home it got pitch dark much more quickly than we had expected. And, of course, down on the level of the lake we could see no farmhouses or any light to guide us.

We knew there was an opening in the ice in the middle of the lake, an opening that ducks would keep free until well into December. But we had always made it a point never to go near it in daylight. On this night we veered far enough off to the side to avoid it, and then, getting tired from skating so far, we sat down to smoke some cigarettes one of the boys had with him. No one could see us out there, so we knew we were safe.

And then the ice began cracking under us.

One of the boys cried out, "Look! There's the opening." We were sitting on the lake right next to it. We had lost our bearings and skated right to it. Had one of us gone in, all of us would have gone and no one would have gotten out, because we were wearing heavy clothes and heavy boots and skates. We couldn't have pulled ourselves out of the water and no one would have heard us call.

We were really scared. We flattened out and

pulled our way across to thicker ice, and headed for home as fast as our skates could take us.

And now — now I would never skate again.

Would I roam the prairies again the way my younger brother Harold and I had done for so many years? We would trap gophers for farmers. Some kids got a penny a tail, but we did it just for fun. And I had always been one to take a dare. If there was any mischief to get into at school, I was first volunteer. Someone dared me to ride my horse right into the school one day before the teacher got there. And I did it, too, but my horse did not like it at all. He wheeled and out we went in a hurry.

I was fearless like that and seldom thought of my own safety. One time Mother had asked me to go down to the mine on our property to get some coal. We had a rule that no one ever went in by himself; but since Mother needed the coal, I went down. We had tracks and a coal car on a winch. We'd take the car into the mine, move it down one of the side runs into a labyrinth of rooms carved out by the miners who had taken most of the coal originally. I went into the first room and dug and loaded my ton of coal and had it pulled out so I could take it home.

The next day I returned to the same room

and found that the whole ceiling, everything, had caved in. It could so easily have happened when I was in there digging. This was one of the closest calls I had had and I learned a little caution that day.

Living out on the farm, we were free to do many things. We always had guns and could shoot at anything we wanted to and as far as we wanted. We couldn't hit anybody else's property because everyone lived so far apart.

Would I ever hunt again? I'd spent a lot of time hunting since my brother had gone away to high school. I didn't go because I never received an eighth grade diploma. I should have gotten it, because I passed the state examination; but just at that time a new course called "Our State" was required, and no diplomas were to be given to students without it. The order had come about the middle of the term; and because I didn't get through the course, I never got my diploma. They told me I would have to stay another year in eighth grade just to get that one subject. Oversized for my grade already, I just stayed home and went to work.

In the winter I would trap weasels, skunks, mink and other small animals to earn extra money. I made enough hunting and working with threshing crews pitching bundles to buy a good saddle horse — one of the best in that whole country. I paid $40 for it and that was a lot of money for one horse at that time. Then I earned enough to buy my own car. I paid over $200 for one of those early Fords that you could repair just by stopping at anybody's fence and taking a piece of wire and wiring it together. But now I'd never drive again.

Would I ever ride my horse or help round up wild horses or help try to break them? Would I ever put on my boxing gloves again? Would I ever run that mile and a half to our mailbox to keep in top physical condition? These thoughts kept going through my mind all the time. What would be the outcome of my life now?

I was confused. I didn't know which way to turn. I tried never to let my family know about my inner feelings; I met everyone with a smile, even though inwardly I was full of grief and fear.

And then the question, "Is there a God?" kept entering my mind. I had been baptized as a child. In fact, much of our home life centered around the Bible and our church. I remember from the time I was about six years old the preparations that were made for the family to get ready to attend church. Shoes had to be cleaned and polished, for no Camp went to church with dirty shoes. Then on Sunday morning my dad inspected us all.

Sunday was the highlight of the week. During this time there were only a few cars in the country and we always drove our horses and buggy to church. Everyone did. There were all kinds of buggies from fancy surreys to the common buckboard. In our family, Sunday school was not just a place to go to see our friends. We had Sunday school study books and my folks made sure that we studied our lesson properly before Sunday. During the church service, all our family sat in the same pew and there was no whispering or shuffling of feet. Dad sat on one end of the pew and Mother on the other.

We had always had daily devotions and prayer at home. I can remember so well how Dad would read from Isaiah and the Psalms and then read through the New Testament. But he always came back to Isaiah and the Psalms, his favorite passages. And we would have prayer every night and morning. Mother wouldn't let us go off to school without it.

Ours was a Danish settlement, so our church was the Evangelical Danish Lutheran Church. I must have been fifteen when I accepted the Lord Jesus Christ as my personal Savior. Ours was a very conservative church. Every summer we had a young peoples' convention and this is where a lot of us were converted. This was not just a form we used to go through as some go through confirmation or baptism. This was genuine conversion; many really dedicated themselves to Christ and others could see the change in them. Our speakers would really preach the Word and show that we had to accept Christ as personal Savior before God could forgive our sins.

Our minister at that time knew how to show his love for young people and it was not unusual to see as many as twenty or twenty-five fellows and girls in his living room, all kneeling in prayer. And he would come to talk with us individually — it didn't matter where we were — in the barn, cleaning the barn, shoveling manure, plowing, or anything. He would walk out to where we were just to see us. In the fall of the year, when the threshing crews were busy, he would get out with the boys and pitch bundles and work right along with the rest of them. He had a lot of influence on my life.

But now I was not so sure. I would sit on the porch, looking out at the wonders of nature, and the question would keep coming back to me, "Is there a God?" There had to be Someone or Something behind the beautiful things in the sky on a clear North Dakota night — and Someone behind the accident that had happened to me. Surely the universe had not created itself; surely there was a reason and a purpose for everything, for even a pulley and a winch and curbing that could fall on a man.

And then I started to bargain with Him.

"Lord, You got me into this deal, so You can get me out of it. If You will give me the use of my legs again, then I will do Your will and do it gladly. But You've got to make the first move."

For ten years I bargained with God and a spirit of rebellion grew in my heart. I never went into a church. He had to make the first move — not me.

But I did read my Bible.

In the meantime, I worked hard to rehabilitate myself in the best ways I knew how. At that time there were no rehabilitation programs to help a handicapped person along. I began to notice articles in newspapers about paraplegics — those paralyzed from the waist down. The more I read, the more I was convinced that I would never walk again. People gave me literature about different kinds of treatments and cures; and one man, very persistent and positive that it would bring back the use of my legs, tried to sell me an electric blanket.

One of my big hurdles was my inability to

uncross my legs. The muscle spasms were terrible. I had to be tied in bed to lie straight and tied in my wheelchair in order to sit up. After nearly a year of this, my family decided that I should go to the Mayo Clinic in Rochester, Minnesota.

My sister Enger and I took a train to Minneapolis to see a doctor there first. After examining me, he decided that the best thing for me was to have my legs amputated. This I would not consent to, so Enger and I went on to Rochester.

After examining me for several days, the Mayo doctors decided that there was a remote chance that if they could sever some nerves in my inner back, they would relieve a lot of my spasms. This would result in my being able to uncross my legs. After the surgery, which I now understand was entirely new in the United States at that time, Dr. Lamont, a noted surgeon from Scotland, was almost as surprised as I when we saw my legs lying straight.

This may seem a small detail, but now I was able to put on street clothing for the first time in over a year. I could go places and do things that one just does not do when he is clothed only in blankets. I could now plan to accomplish some things on my own.

My life had taken on new meaning and I

was ready to try my new wings. One of the first things I did was to build a framework of parallel bars so that I could support my weight with my arms and try to walk. I would try by the hour to make my feet move, but it was no use. My legs just would not go where I wanted them to. But I kept on trying and trying.

Next, I tried to build a square frame to be used as a crutch that would not tip, but the spasm was still too great in my leg muscles for me to get very far with this.

I knew if I were ever going to be able to walk, I must have strong arms and hands; so I made a cart out of some old buggy wheels with a plow seat between them and handles to make it go. This was during the depression days of the 1930s and we certainly did not have money to buy such things. It turned out to be a strange-looking contraption — those two wheels with a seat between them and that old discarded equipment.

But I was able to wheel this cart as much as half a mile from our farmhouse. It gave me a chance to get away from the house by myself to think. I would go out as far as I dared on the North Dakota prairie, taking my new fox terrier Spot and my twenty-two rifle with me for shooting rabbits and gophers. Wheeling this cart helped develop my arms and shoulders and this was my aim in building it. Admittedly, I had rather difficult going at times; the prairie terrain was rough with numerous gopher holes and dirt mounds. And cattle ranged over this land, leaving evidence that was an added inconvenience.

I would sit by the hour on our front porch and dream about the things that could be done with our farm. I planned everything from raising crops to beef cattle, potatoes, and even chickens. Carefully, I would plan every detail from what the cost would be to what the market would offer. It would take me days to write out every detail. Each new dream would require me to find new costs of material and labor and the possibility of new markets. I would try to sell each idea to my father, but there was barely enough money around to keep us going, let alone to start something new. I felt those dreams and plans were really good for me, however, as they kept my mind alert and my initiative intact.

On summer evenings Harold would come in from the field and we would play catch, since I had now developed my arms and was able to throw a fairly good ball.

We now had an old Whippet car in place of my Model T. Hand controls were unheard of at that time; but I found that I could take a length of board and manipulate the clutch and brake so that I could go driving out on the pasture land.

Even though I had learned to do these things, I found that I still was not satisfied. There must be something else I could do to be independent and to help support myself. People seemed to think that folks in wheelchairs were not meant to do anything. This disgusted me! I even asked our pastor if there were some kind of Christian work I could do, but he gave me to understand that all Christian work was for healthy, able-bodied folk. I remember trying to do some embroidery on dresser scarfs and tea towels for the Ladies Aid Society, just because I felt that they had tried to do so much for me in so many ways.

But it was my father who helped me feel that I was needed. Whenever some of the farm machinery broke down or needed repair, he would bring what he could for me to fix. In showing me that even on the farm I could be of some use, he did the most important thing that anyone can do for a handicapped person. He filled my deep need to know I was useful.

One day Dad was afraid something had gone wrong with the binder, so he just laid the part up on the porch and let me help fix it. It wasn't that he needed any help fixing it. He knew he could take that binder apart with his eyes closed; but he was one of these guys that — well, he never sat and looked at me as if he thought, "Boy, Freddy, I sure feel sorry for you." He never did that, although I know it must have eaten his heart out sometimes to see that I couldn't do the things that I used to.

One day when all in the family were busy and I was alone, I thought it would be an experience to try to get out of my wheelchair and down to the ground by myself. I tried and tried and finally in about half an hour I made it — that is, without just falling out. I was so tired I could hardly move, but I was proud of myself. I have always felt that this was a big step toward my rehabilitation. It was another thing I could do all by myself.

I couldn't wait to show off what I had learned to do; so the next time everyone was working at the back of the house, I got out of my wheelchair and slid the three steps down to the ground from the porch. I got my chair down to the ground, hoisted myself up into it and wheeled back to where they were. They were stunned!

One other time I got myself out of the chair and into a sitting position on the davenport. My father would often come to me, sit down and talk over the depression, the social trends of the day and the political situation. Dad came in just then and stopped in his tracks.

Seeing me there was a real shock to him. It was almost as if he had seen me stand up and walk!

We all were greatly concerned about the farmers, as each day seemed to bring them closer and closer to bankruptcy. He would discuss this with me and when we would hear of relatives coming from out of state to see us, he would always say, "Fred, it would be just as well if we don't let them know how difficult things are with us. Let's just be thankful for what we have."

My mother was always cheerful and always ready to see something amusing in almost any situation. How thankful I was that Mother and Dad and the rest of my family never gave me the "Poor Freddie" look.

The young people of the Trinity, Zion, and Norma Lutheran churches will never know how much they helped me over the rough spots those first few years. They would take turns coming to visit me every so often. Sometimes as many as thirty-five or forty would come to our house for a get-together. I anxiously looked forward to their visits and remember with much pleasure these very happy times. We really had a ball!

Young people can be of great service to the handicapped by taking time to just stop and chat as they would with able-bodied friends.

The winter months seemed so long. This was the time I dreaded most. I remember once there were five weeks when I was not able to go any place. We were snowed in and, of course, no one could come to see me either. The coldest it got was 55 below zero and the warmest was 24 below.

One who comforted me most during these times was Spot. I really believe every handicapped person should have a pet of some kind. I spent many happy hours with him, throwing balls for him to bring back and teaching him many little tricks. When I took afternoon naps, Spot was supposed to stay in another room, but I would call him and he would make one big jump, land on the throw rug in front of the door, slide all the way over to my bed, then up he would come in one joyful bound.

The winters would finally pass and spring would bring welcome release.

3

Our Move to Minot

For two years Mother and Dad and I lived alone on the farm. My older brothers Albert and Dan had gone to Minnesota to work. My younger brother Harold was living in Minot where Enger was living while she worked at the hospital. Both Ella and Lydia had gone back to Portland, Oregon, to work. My folks were past sixty-five years of age and it was a quiet time at home for me.

They were both devoted Christians and they spent time reading their Bibles and praying. After all was quiet at night, father would kneel beside his chair before he mounted the stairs to go to bed and he would pray for each one of us. He knew the Lord would provide for our needs and he claimed Romans 8:28 for our guiding light: "And we know that all things work together for good to them that love God, to them who are the called according to his purpose." Mother would quote Romans 8:31, "If God be for us, who can be against us?" Although I did not realize it then, I was greatly influenced by their faith.

Then, suddenly, my father suffered a cerebral hemorrhage. He was sick only a few hours. He passed away on December 23. He would have had his 66th birthday on Christmas Day. On the 27th, I entered a church for the first time since my accident. We laid him to rest in the church cemetery near people he had loved so well.

I loved my father deeply.

I remember when during the winter months of my early childhood he would read and virtually memorize a novel — one of the limited few he had access to at that time. We would all wait anxiously for him to complete it, because we knew we were in for a treat. He would build a good fire in our old coal stove and, as all my brothers and sisters would sit around him, would tell us the story in his own way and make us feel we had read the book ourselves.

Many times as a youngster I would try to go to the dinner table without washing properly. Dad wouldn't say a word about it but would go ahead with the table blessing. Then he would inform me that there was nothing for me to eat until I had washed my hands properly. Everyone else would go ahead and eat while I would go out to wash and comb my hair. Dad was particular; my hands had to be really clean.

My dad always thought if something was worth doing, it was worth doing well. If I wanted to go somewhere in the evening, I would have to milk my cows and do my chores first. I would finish quickly. But Dad knew how much milk I should get from the cows; and when I would get through in too big a hurry, he would milk my cows again and usually get as much milk as I had the first time. I would rather he had taken me behind the woodshed.

Butchering a beef was a big day at our home. Even now I can almost see Dad and Mother as they cut up the meat and put choice pieces aside to take to some elderly people who lived next to our church, to a widow who was also under my folk's watchful eye, and to the pastor's house.

Dad's Homegoing left a big decision to be made within our family. Now what would we do, my mother and I? She couldn't run the farm and certainly I was not capable. The farm had not been on a paying basis and accumulated taxes stood against it. There was nothing we could do but lose the farm because the taxes could not be paid.

The only course open to us was to go to Minot to live with Enger and Harold. Lydia came back from Portland, and she and Enger decided to run a boarding house in Minot. Not one of us was happy with the location of the place they rented. I didn't like it because it was on a second floor and up three flights of steps. We lived there only a short time before Lydia and Enger found a large house to rent. Beside the boarding business they were also equipped to offer sleeping rooms. I moved in with them.

It was a long time before I could bring myself to go out on the porch and even longer before I would venture out on the sidewalks. A handicapped person in North Dakota then was indeed a soul by himself, confined to a house and four walls and expected to stay there. During these years I did not become acquainted with another handicapped person, and I was very much alone. People just did not expect me to become self-supporting much less to have as vital an interest in life as they did. Wheelchairs were bulky and inconvenient and really useful only to transfer a person from bed to chair or just provide a place where he would exist until it was time to go to bed again.

My friends couldn't understand why I wanted strong muscles and a feeling of independence. They couldn't understand why I should want to be alone at different times in order to study out a problem. They were just not prepared to accept a handicapped person on their own level in everyday life, much less in business. This was vividly borne out when Franklin Roosevelt was elected president of the United States. A person very close to me said dogmatically, "A man in a wheelchair just should not be allowed to become the president of the United States under any condition."

President Roosevelt's ability was not measured by the use of his body but by his mind and will and character. I feel his popularity in later elections and his ability as a leader were ample evidence of the degree to which he had conquered his physical handicap. His political party affiliations had no part in my admiration of him, but he was a marked example to me of what heights a man could reach who did not let his handicaps conquer him.

Finally I met several men in Minot who played checkers and this was the turning point in my life. At first I wasn't able to win any games; and nearly every time I was beaten, I would have such a worthless feeling. Why, I couldn't even play checkers! But I felt that I couldn't let that go on, so I decided to study checkers and master the game. No mere game was going to beat *me*. I got books by some of the great checker masters and studied their moves. Back in my mind was the hope that maybe I could become one of the "greats" and that this might lead to a self-supporting life.

I studied the game by the hour and soon I was a winning player. Not long afterward, I learned I could play three or four players at one time if I would concentrate on the games. Then I found I could play blindfolded and still win. I played some of North Dakota's greatest checker players. My greatest thrill was playing the renowned Willie Ryan, third best player in the world at that time.

Once, when we checker players heard a "new man" had moved into town from the East Coast, we found it was hard to contact him. He would walk to work across from our house every day and we didn't want to make it appear that we were anxious to play him. So every evening we would sit on our porch and play about the time he would be going home. Soon his attention was drawn to us and he came down our side of the street. We offered to play a game with him and the amusing thing was that he really beat us. He played an entirely different game approach from the kind we were used to playing.

We were forced to analyze his game — and then we were top men again!

We traveled around the state and played with different checker groups who challenged us. I played in the Northwest Tournament and came out second. I enjoyed checkers so much and became so engrossed in each game that I would lie awake for hours at night and mentally replay each game I didn't win. I soon came to realize that this was not the kind of life I wanted to live, because I could not seem to play for fun only. I stopped competing.

Living in Minot proved to me that many things are needed in public places if handicapped people are to take part in the daily routine of able-bodied people. I realized that the buildings had not been designed with the needs of the handicapped in mind. Steps were everywhere. Curbs were high. Dentists' and doctors' offices were too often upstairs. Doors were too narrow. Rest rooms were not suitable for use. It seemed that everywhere I went I was faced with new problems. It almost made me stay home.

But I enjoyed the company of the girls from the hospital. They often would come to go with me to the theater or out to dinner, but always I would have to fight steps or curbs or other obstacles. All the members of my family had become expert in handling a wheel-chair, so I had never realized how difficult it was for "people on the outside" to manage one. I remember so clearly the day a lady wanted to help me into our house. She didn't know how and I didn't realize it. I assumed she would grasp the back of my chair as I went over the threshhold to enter, but instead she just stood behind me. I raised my small front wheels by gripping the hand-rims to start our move — and over I went, backwards. I landed on the floor at her feet! It must have been funny to see and even I was amused, once I was sure I was not hurt. I guess this was really the first girl I ever "fell" for — even though she was old enough to be my mother.

I learned a lot about people in Minot. I learned what it was like to have people around constantly. I learned what it was like to live in a boarding house, to play checkers com-petitively, to win, to lose, and to try a small business venture. I wanted to get involved in an enterprise I could carry on from my chair, and so I took up working in leather on bill-folds and key chains. But all enterprise is not production, and I learned that I was not able to estimate a salesman's worth. I used up all the money I had for supplies, made my products, and gave them to the leathercraft salesman to sell. I never heard from the man again. This was a hard lesson for me, but a valuable one.

Another thing I tried that proved to be of inestimable value was working with younger people. Harold and I were the youngest members of our family and I had really never had much contact with younger people. But the large house in Minot was next to an Episcopal church where the rector was quite concerned for large groups of teen-age boys who played near the church. He had no proper place for them to play nor anyone to be with them.

He came to me one day and asked me to supervise their play. What a joy it was to be needed! We arranged competitive sports and entertainments for them. These boys were not members of the church families and most of them came from broken homes. Here I got a special feel for the needs of another group of people, and I enjoyed working and becoming friends with boys I had never known before. Really, they did more for me than I ever did for them.

But times were changing for us again. Lydia decided to go back to Portland, Oregon, and Enger was to be married; so the boarding house was closed. This left Harold, mother, and me alone. Harold drove a truck for a stockyard and earned our living, so we moved to a smaller apartment. Life just seemed to "go along," but it was hard for Harold to keep us on his salary. Mother felt this and decided to go to Portland to see Ella and Lydia, who also had married by this time.

One Sunday morning Harold and I were sitting at the breakfast table.

"Fred," he said, "I've got an idea. Why don't we move to Portland too?"

"Okay by me," I said. "There's not very much to keep us in Minot."

So we packed up our belongings and in a week's time were en route to Portland on the train.

Even this offered many obstacles as Harold had to carry me not only onto the train but everywhere we went during our trip. He was always my legs and carried me to the dining car, rest room, sleeping compartment and everywhere I needed to go.

So here we were in September 1939, moving across the northern plains into the Pacific Northwest. Who could know how different life was going to be for me now!

4

West to Portland

On our arrival in Portland, my sister Lydia and her husband Merle Grounds invited us to move in with them. Harold was fortunate enough to get a job in a lumber company office within three days. I was impatient to begin to do something too, but jobs were nonexistent for a handicapped person and no place was equipped to employ anyone in a wheelchair.

Merle and Lydia sensed my anxiety to be out and doing, and so they made a deliberate effort to take me with them whenever they went out in the car, even to the store. It seemed no problem at all for Merle to pick me up and carry me from one place to another. He always seemed to have time for me and the inclination to want me to go with him and enjoy myself on these trips. His getting me out of the house and into the city really helped me. I now wanted to meet new people and to get on in the world.

But I still kept up my quiet time. I had through the years consistently read my Bible, for it was my part of that bargain I had made with the Lord. One day as I was reading, I came across an old familiar verse, Matthew 6:33: "Seek ye *first* the kingdom of God, and his righteousness, and all these things shall be added unto you." I reread the verse. I read it again and then many, many times.

At last I began to think perhaps I had been going about my rehabilitation all wrong. Maybe I hadn't put the power on the right end. Here I had been sitting for ten years, waiting for God to act. He had been active all the time, but I was the one who was dormant.

But how, I wondered, should I go about putting this verse to work? I had prayed for a business, a job, a wife and a family, but I had never believed God would answer my prayers. How should I start?

First, I knew I had to get some clothes other than overall pants in order to be presentable. Money was something I did not have; but by using all available cash, I did raise seven dollars which I used to buy a second-hand suit. You see, I had decided that I must do this by myself.

Then, if I were to "seek first the kingdom of God," where better could I go than to a church? This had to be one that I could go to by myself, as the church is God's house and these visits must be on my own. I knew there was a church only a few blocks away, so I went there, wheeling my chair down the street. It was not until I got there that I found the first obstacle — ten steps led up to the sanctuary! This first Sunday was going to be quite an experience, I thought, until several ushers discovered me and came to my assistance. I just left it up to them to decide how to get me inside. How they pulled and tugged, trying to get me up those steps! After this, I equipped my chair with some handles, so all the men had to do was pick the chair up and carry it up the steps.

I began to like the people there; they were really a devoted group of Christians. Soon I was attending Sunday school and church regularly. Like so many others, this church always seemed to be in need of teachers in the Sunday school. They badly needed a teacher for a group of junior high boys and I volunteered. I had no experience with anything of the sort and I had no idea about how to plan and teach a lesson.

The first Sunday morning as I went to teach, I went with mixed emotions. I was not at all sure I should be teaching or that I was even capable of presenting God's Word. I don't know how I got through the first lesson; I was so filled with doubt and tension that I was wet with perspiration before it was over. I think it was just as strange for the boys to have someone in a wheelchair teaching them as it was for me to be there.

Although I wasn't aware of it at the time, this was the church's problem class. At first I too had a discipline problem; but in a few weeks, that righted itself in a kind of funny way. I brought a jar to church one Sunday and we had an election. One boy was elected sergeant-at-arms and his job was to keep order. If anyone spoke out of turn or said something not pertaining to the lesson, it cost him a penny. If someone came without his Bible, it cost him a nickel; and if he missed a Sunday, it was a dime. The boys thought this was fun and our new sergeant-at-arms enforced the rules.

One boy in particular gave me a bad time for a while. He was not a bad boy, but just active and full of mischief. One Sunday morning I thought I was doing very well, because everyone was paying attention, especially this one boy. He sat there looking down, taking in every word I was saying — or so I thought. I said to myself, "Now, I've finally gotten to him." I believe I would have reached around and patted myself on the back if it had been possible.

But I was wrong. He looked up at me and said, "Mr. Camp, how many pairs of shoes do you wear out in a year?" I don't believe he had heard one word I had been teaching.

I do have fond memories of this class though. We grew so much that our room would hardly allow enough seating, and then we grew some more and just had to let the boys sit on the floor.

One Sunday morning, the church school decided to take a collection for a particular missionary. Each class was to see how much it could raise for this project. We had all our money from fines and the boys decided to give that to the missionary. It turned out that our class gave more than all the other classes put together. I wish you could have seen those boys' faces! I don't think there was a prouder group of boys in Portland.

One other time when one of our congregation's young men was in the armed forces during World War II, my boys decided to send him a New Testament with all our names in it. The pastor not only agreed that it was a good idea, but to our surprise, just before he delivered his sermon that Sunday morning, he held up the Testament and explained what the class had done. Again they were very pleased with their work. I never had a better class of young boys! After we sent this one Testament, the older youth groups picked up the project and started to send Testaments to all our servicemen all over the world.

One memorable day about this time, Harold came home from a sporting goods store with some trout fishing flies. I looked at those flies and it came to me so plainly, "Here is something I could do in a wheelchair and at home!"

"Mack," I said to my brother's friend who was visiting us at the time, "who tied these?"

His reply was, "I know a man who will show you how to tie, I'm sure. He's a Mr. Dollbeer and he works for the Portland firemen."

So I contacted Mr. Dollbeer. Yes, he would be glad to help me, but it would take eleven or twelve dollars for materials to start. Well, I didn't have one dollar, not to mention twelve; but I was determined to tie flies.

I would sell greeting cards to get the money. This was a hard thing for me to do, as I could never sell on the street without feeling that each sale was a kind of charity gift from the buyer. I don't know why I felt this way, but I just could not shake the feeling. I wheeled up and down the street, asking every lady I saw working in her yard if I could show her my card samples. I finally made $11.50 and promptly quit the card business. I called Mr. Dollbeer again, he came out to see me, and I was in the fly business.

I got some fly patterns and copied them. I also got whatever help I could from other fly tyers. One man who was especially helpful was Earl Poulsen. He was already in the business and he helped me with business connections.

Soon I was receiving orders and selling all I could make, but hooks were a big problem. The war had cut off the supplies from Norway, where most of the hooks were made, when the German army took over that country. So I started to sell only to a dealer who could supply me with the same number of hooks that I sold him in the finished form. The arrangement really worked. So my prayers were answered again! Now I had a business — not a big one, but a good start. I needed help only in bookkeeping and letter writing.

Now that I was making a small amount of money from the sale of my flies, I decided to construct a motorized wheelchair in order to make it easier and quicker to travel on the streets and to go to the ball park. I had laid out all my plans on paper and knew exactly what I needed to do the job. I spent long hours when I was tired from fly-tying to accomplish this job. But accomplish it, I did — and it worked! Actually, all I did was put a small Briggs and Stratton engine under my chair seat. I used a slip clutch and a small wheel in front with a guide bar. I now made a lot of noise but I could go faster. All this proved quite an attraction to the people on the street. Men and women, boys and girls all took turns trying my wheelchair out. If they got it first, I had to wait my turn; but I felt I had taken another important step. Again I had done something to help myself — and it felt good!

Another group I enjoyed very much was a ball club of 15-year-old boys, many of whom were in my "problem" Sunday school class. We asked the Park Board for a place to play regularly and Westmoreland Park was assigned to us at certain times for a regular softball diamond. We organized our boys and they really worked. They played ball and they played hard. Every practice found them all in attendance. I managed the team and worked with each one in the particular way he needed to become better at his position.

A competition was organized and a league formed. We played all teams who challenged us. At the end of the season we came out second in our league; but best of all, we came out with a group of boys who had become fine sportsmen, ones who knew what it was to put the team before themselves.

One time we were in particularly high spirits. We were challenged by a men's team. Their competition had not shown up, so they came over to our diamond and wanted us to play them. We certainly surprised them by beating them soundly. Our pitcher was following my instructions to the letter and he held the adult team to one run.

Again I felt the elation of doing something worthwhile even though I was in a wheelchair. I was so proud of my boys. I began to feel that at last I was putting the "Seek ye first the kingdom of God" verse into action. Every time I talked to one of the boys, I tried to put across more of my Bible teaching and live out the lessons I myself had learned.

Even some of the problem boys were thinking about their spiritual lives. Was this what God wanted me to do? Was I pleasing Him with my actions when I was with these boys? Was I being the kind of a teacher and leader He would want me to be? All these questions filled my mind and I worked all the harder to learn His way through daily Bible reading and study.

5

The Chin-Up Club

During these first few years in Portland, I started to get acquainted with other handicapped people. One girl in particular was Beth Sellwood, who wanted to start a club for handicappers. She invited four or five of us together and we started what is known today as the "Chin-Up Club."

I can't praise Beth enough. What a girl she was! When we talked about being handicapped, we just didn't know how handicapped she was. She wrote letters by the hundreds; but in order to write, she had to take one hand to guide the other on the page. She could not close her eyes; day and night her lids remained open. Her lips did not move when she talked; she could only lower her jaw. Were it not for a body brace, she could not have sat up. And many, many of her days were spent in bed or on a stretcher.

Beth contacted the handicapped wherever she heard of them. Her father and mother took her to visit those who could not go out in a group. She encouraged the lame, the blind, the deaf, and all degrees of handicapped people to band together to share one another's problems, to enjoy the company of others, and to know the benefits of close contact with other handicapped persons.

Many people who had lived as prisoners within four walls began to get out and get together. Many parents and adults began to see that other families had bigger and more complicated problems. Just the meetings that we called parties were very beneficial. Many people who had never been in a group came, and many went away feeling that maybe they weren't as handicapped as they had always thought they were. Many found that people would accept them as persons despite their wheelchair, crutches, stretcher, braces, and deformities, and the nonhandicapped began to forget the fact that their newfound friends were a bit different from their able-bodied friends. Many times since, I have heard people say, "You know, you just forget that that person is in a chair when you really get to know him."

People came to these parties from all over the Portland area and then from the outlying districts. Soon many came from 100 or 200 or even 300 miles away. Beth's speech defect kept her from taking charge of such a gathering so I found myself elected master of ceremonies on these occasions. Soon we were having 150 to 200 people once a month in some hall in Portland for pot luck dinners and visiting and for some type of entertainment which was usually not of a professional quality, but was just presented by our amateur club members or their families.

I found my pleasure in seeking out those particular people who really needed to know others with a handicap. These were the ones I spent my time with, and soon I began to see each one of them gradually becoming more and more at ease with other people. Then came the time when I would see or hear one of them showing signs of rehabilitation, signs of wanting to take an active part with friends and neighbors, signs of beginning to feel that he was not just a person shut away but one who had come out into the sunshine of life. To me, this was true rehabilitation! When this happened, I couldn't stop until I found a bit of time to look heavenward and say, "Father, thank You again."

I think particularly of a tiny eight-year-old

blondie, a pretty little girl who had been a spastic since birth. She had never been away from her home; so I went there to visit her and ask her parents to bring her to a party. She was lying there on a stretcher, and I am sure that this was the way she had spent every day since she was born.

Her parents did bring her to the party and I was there to greet her. I will never forget the look of fright on her face as she clung to my hand and watched the other handicapped people enjoy the afternoon. It was nearly two hours later when she finally gained enough courage to let go of my hand and observe the happenings on her own for the rest of the afternoon.

I wish I could tell of all the wonderful people I have met through Chin-Up Club. I wish I could make people understand how many members had almost insurmountable problems and yet found that association with people cleared the clouds away from their lives. It would take volumes to detail each life, for I have found that every handicapped person is a special story all in himself.

At our meetings for entertainment, we would put on our own impromptu acts. We would hear about someone who sang or played an instrument or performed in some other manner and would call on him to "help" us.

Many of these people had never been before a microphone. Several regular performers would accompany the new ones the first time, and we found much hidden talent. We were delighted that this seemed to be such a successful way to bring people out of themselves, for often the performer would gain confidence he had never known before.

Spontaneous pranks often livened our gatherings and I must confess that I was the perpetrator of many of them. I had a motive beyond just having fun, for it was often a bit of practical joking that brought a handicapped person out of his shell.

At one of our conventions, when I was master of ceremonies, I asked my friend Bill Judd, who has a beautiful voice, to lead the song, "God Bless America." I had instigated so many pranks that our people knew a chance when they saw one; and you can guess what happened. No one sang except Bill Judd and me! Next day, the newspaper said that Bill Judd and Fred Camp sang a duet. This duet was my first — and last. If it hadn't been for Bill's voice, I don't know what I would have done. I'm not much of a singer and I just kind of sneaked in on a few tones!

Many of the handicapped are musically gifted, though, and I think that perhaps the most divine voice I ever heard was that of a man completely paralyzed from his neck down. He had been bedfast for years. When we went to visit him in his home, he spent a pleasant time with us, helping us all in so many ways to realize how fortunate we were even though we were handicapped. And then he sang the "Lord's Prayer" and we taped it for a radio program. Here indeed was one of God's choice people. One could feel the presence of God's love in his room.

6

Bea

At the 1944 annual convention of the Chin-Up Club in Salem, Oregon, I had the honor of crowning president and founder Beth Sellwood our Queen of Courage. As I was coming down from the platform in my wheelchair, I noticed someone had dropped a yellow rose from a bouquet. Since several girls in wheelchairs were sitting at the front of the convention room, I picked up the yellow rose and gave it a toss in their direction. It landed in the lap of Bernice Nightingale.

Before the day was over, I had become acquainted with Bea. I noticed that she had strong and unaffected hands, and soon I found that she was interested in doing some kind of work. I discussed fly-tying with her and found she would like to learn how to do it.

But I lived in Portland and she lived in Stayton, some sixty miles away. Teaching her to tie flies would involve some difficulty, as one must learn the basics before it is possible to go ahead professionally.

To get started, Bea came to Portland to my fly shop in my sister's basement. When she was doing quite well, we arranged that I would go to Stayton on weekends. On Saturdays, a bus driver would help me aboard in Portland, put my chair on the bus, and take me to Stayton. Since the bus went within two blocks of Bea's home, he would detour and take me off the bus, along with my chair, right in front of her house. Bea's sister often came to Stayton from Portland to see her parents and I often managed a ride back with her and her husband, or I again contacted my much appreciated bus driver.

As Bea's fly-tying improved, I suddenly became aware that some of these trips I was taking were really not necessary. But I had become interested in Bea as a person, for I had found someone to whom I could talk about almost anything. The fact that both she and I were paraplegic was common ground for a discussion of our feelings and likes and interest in handicapped people. She understood the things that I had not been able to get anyone to understand before.

Those were good days — days when we could bring our pent-up feelings into the open and discuss our personal problems.

I had met many girls before, even girls who were very attractive to me; but somehow my physical condition always presented a barrier. I had always felt that a man in a wheelchair just shouldn't consider marriage. And I had never before been able to provide financially for a wife. But somehow with Bea, my former convictions about "no marriage while in a chair" just didn't seem important. The honest fact is that it never even worried me. I knew she understood my paraplegia and I also understood hers.

After practicing a few weeks she began to produce salable flies, and one day I phoned to give her an order for fifty dozen of a new pattern. She tackled the order thinking she knew what I meant; but when she finished, I saw that all fifty dozen were tied wrong. We couldn't throw them out; hooks were still hard to get, for this was during World War II. I hated to ask her to cut the fly from each hook and start again, but it was my only alternative. I have always wondered just what she thought of me as she cut the material from the hooks; I know it must not have been good! But really, it didn't hurt our relationship one bit.

Weeks passed and Bea's fly-tying improved even more. Each time we met and talked, we seemed to have an especially good time, and I enjoyed becoming more and more acquainted with her. She learned to know my likes and dislikes in so many ways. I happen to be very fond of apple pie, and each time I arrived at the Nightingale residence, it seemed that apple pie was the special dessert of the day. You know, somehow I thought Bea was making those pies; but I finally found out her mother was the baker. Better apple pie just couldn't be found.

Each time I went to see Bea or each time she came to Portland should have allowed us time to be alone. But somehow things just didn't work that way. Between her family and my family, someone was always keeping us company. In fact, Bea's youngest sister Edith was the proverbial shadow — always right there. No one seemed to sense that we would enjoy just being alone. Finally, I decided that Bea must have some special fly-tying instructions that just could not be interrupted, and we were able to have some unforgettable times when we could talk and share so many of our own personal thoughts.

I soon began to realize that God was still answering my prayers and that He must have said yes to my prayers for a wife and home.

Now I could see that my relationship with Bea was not to be just a friendly one, but that Bea was the one I wanted to marry.

Lydia and her husband were amazed when I told them we were planning to be married.

Merle said, "And to think all this happened right here under our noses, and we never suspected a thing!" He and Lydia took me shopping and I purchased a diamond ring and wedding band.

People had many different reactions to our engagement:

"Two people in wheelchairs shouldn't get married!"

"So what if they do get engaged. Nothing will ever come from such a relationship."

"They'll just be a double burden for someone to care for if they marry."

In the meantime we made plans. We found a better market for our trout flies and leaders. We worked tirelessly early and late, planning our home, planning our furniture, planning the needs of all of our household, planning how we could make all of our dreams come true.

Still it seemed difficult for us to spend time together. I had to go by bus or car to Stayton and she had to get her parents to bring her to Portland. Those were the years of gas rationing, and transportation was limited; so we decided on a short engagement and began to look for a house to buy in Stayton, because a small town offered grocery stores, hardware stores, banks, doctors, post offices, restaurants, and drug stores all within a few blocks.

We heard of a large seven-room house for sale just two blocks from downtown and went to see it. It needed much repair, being one of the oldest houses in Stayton. But its having only two steps in front meant it could be ramped easily, so it seemed well suited to our needs. The purchase was made and our wedding date was set for June 23rd, about three weeks away.

We had time to make the place liveable, but first we had to have a ramp built. I decided that that was a thing I could do by myself. There were some good wooden planks and two-by-fours at the back of the house, so I began to work. It was quite a job from a wheelchair! The ramp was to be thirty feet long and three feet wide. Once I formed the framework, it took thirty pieces of three-foot planking to build it; and I cut every one with a hand saw. It seemed each time I pushed the saw forward I pushed my wheelchair back. I was indeed one tired guy when night came!

But soon the ramp was completed and we could more easily get in and out to do the housecleaning, the wallpapering and painting. I quickly came to appreciate the fact that Bea was one of eight children and that she had several aunts and uncles. Everyone came! They cleaned, they painted, they wallpapered. They gave us floor coverings for wedding presents and laid them for us. We'll never forget those days.

As the time drew near for our wedding, all my Chin-Up friends in Portland became aware that it was really going to happen — I actually *was* going to get married! They planned a surprise shower at the regularly scheduled party and Bea and I never once suspected that it was to be especially for us. When people began to arrive, everyone seemed laden with gifts. Still we were not aware of just what was going on. As master of ceremonies I was on the platform. Several numbers on the program had been given, when suddenly four men lifted Bea's chair and brought her up beside me. Someone took the mike out of my hand and people came from a side room bringing gifts for us. We were speechless.

The new master of ceremonies announced our wedding plans and the rest of the program was dedicated to us. We received everything we needed to begin a home — dishes, silver, linen, blankets, kitchenware, pictures, keepsakes from dear friends, glassware, clocks.

Many of these things still grace our home after twenty-five years. When Bea and I regained our composure, we invited them all to come to the wedding at the Methodist Church in Stayton on the evening of June 23.

Our wedding day arrived, and with it a host of friends and relatives. They filled the church to overflowing. We treasure the memory of other wheelchairs, crutches, canes and stretchers, all bearing dear friends who came to congratulate us as we started life together.

My brother Dan was best man and Bea's attendants were three of her sisters, Florence, Esther and Shirley. I remember waiting at the front of the church with Dan as the ceremony started. I could hardly sit there quietly. And then I saw Bea coming down the aisle in her wheelchair and I was no longer nervous. She was dressed in pure white net over taffetta, full formal length. Yellow roses and white gardenias adorned the white Bible in her lap. It is a picture I will never forget.

We have always treasured the special songs. "Always" was beautifully sung by my friend Al Rosium, an arthritic. All his joints are stiffened so much that he can only stand or lie down. Bea's sister Shirley sang "At Dawning." Pastor Cookingham went through the whole ceremony without notes. He confessed later that he also was a bit nervous — never before in all his years in the ministry had he officiated at a wedding where both bride and groom were in wheelchairs!

A reception followed the ceremony, and everyone was so gracious.

Helen Hoover, staff writer from the Portland *Oregonian,* and two photographers had asked to be permitted to take pictures of our wedding and write our story. Knowing the encouragement it could be to handicapped readers everywhere, we consented. All were very considerate during the ceremony and the reception. The June 25 edition of the *Oregonian* carried three pictures and the story of our wheelchair wedding on the front page. It shared news space with the announcement of President Truman's arrival in Portland for a brief visit.

Our article read:

"Stayton went to a wedding Saturday night, but it was no ordinary wedding that brought the people crowding into the Methodist church.

"When the minister's words were finished, pronouncing them man and wife, Fred Camp of Portland and his bride, the former Bernice Nightingale of Stayton, kissed each other across the intervening chromium bars of their two wheelchairs.

"Before them lay the promise of a full and happy life which probably neither dreamed possible when, at identical periods in their youth — just before their 18th birthdays — almost identical injuries had made it impossible for either ever to walk again.

Home Awaits Couple

"Fred and Bernice Camp went from the marriage ceremony, and a gala reception in the gift-packed basement of the church, to the home they have bought and furnished, a rambling, seven-room house under maples near the Santiam river. There, with his workroom in one wing, Camp will earn their living with his sportsmen's supply business. His wife will relinquish her career as city treasurer and mimeographer-typist to keep house.

"Seated in the wheelchairs, without which they cannot move from place to place, the Camps greeted not only their Slayton friends, but also many members of Oregon's famous Chin-Up Club.

"It is unlikely Fred and Bernice would ever have met but for the Chin-Up Club. Under the conviction that no one needs to be lonely or idle, no matter how cruel his physical handicap, the Chin-Uppers organized themselves several years ago and have sought aggressively to win to membership the afflicted men, women and children throughout the state, that they may pool their sympathies and talents for a fuller life.

Two Meet in Salem

"Camp and his wife met at the Chin-Uppers' annual gathering in Salem last June, where she was secretary and he was master of ceremonies. They found one common bond immediately. Camp's back had been broken 16 years ago when a pulley fell on him while he was working in a well. His legs paralyzed, he made a wheelchair his means of locomotion, his hands his means of support. His home was at 5915 SE 22nd Avenue, Portland, with his mother, Mrs. Anna Camp.

"He learned to make fishing flies and leaders, and built up a clientele which extends throughout the northwest. At Moreland Presbyterian church, he was popular as the teacher of a Sunday school class, and at Chin-Up affairs, he always has been chosen as a master of ceremonies.

"His wife suddenly faced an entire readjustment of her life six years ago when shortly after graduation from high school she fell headlong from a tree, fracturing her spine.

Wife Learns Trade

"At their meeting last June, Camp offered to teach her his trade. She learned well, serving her apprenticeship in Portland while staying with a sister.

"The new Mrs. Camp has deft fingers, and will help her husband fill his orders for fishing flies. He employs three other persons as assistants, and in keeping with club purposes, these are Chin-Uppers too.

"The Camps' was the second wedding to grow out of Chin-Up friendships. Last April, Bill Judd of Milwaukie and Opal Berlincourt of Albany were married."

It was gratifying to receive letters and clippings throughout the next few months from every state in the Union, from Hawaii, from Mexico, Canada, Germany, and Italy. Each told how the senders happened to read the articles and why they were taking the trouble to send us the clippings. These clippings have become treasured keepsakes.

At 11:30 p.m. we arrived at our new home. I need not report that I did not carry Bea over the threshhold. But when everyone had gone and we were alone, we stopped everything to thank God for such a wonderful chance to live our lives to His honor and glory and to ask Him to be the Head of our household from that time forward.

Now God had given me a business, a wife and a home, and a new life to live. I was so grateful, for I knew that when God answered prayer He never did it halfway. My heart filled with the hope that I would be the kind of husband, the kind of businessman, the kind of man He wanted me to be in our future together.

7

Two Lives Become One

Sunday morning the sun came up early on our first day of married life. We decided it was time to get up, have breakfast at leisure, and go to church as was the habit of us both. We attended the same church that had been so festively decorated at our wedding the evening before; for since the time she accepted Christ as her Lord and Savior at age fourteen, soon after she had come to Oregon from South Dakota, Bea's spiritual life had been connected with this church. She knew these people and considered them all part of her spiritual family. Here she had helped with Sunday school classes and been in youth groups before her back injury when she was seventeen; and here she had attended ever since then, whenever possible.

I think the whole congregation was amazed to see us wheeling those ten blocks to church that Sunday morning. I know we got a great blessing out of showing God our gratefulness in this manner.

We did not go on a honeymoon immediately. We had so many new ways to get accustomed to. Neither of us had lived away from our families since our injuries; so we found many new things we had to learn to do to care for ourselves physically and to accomplish the household duties of cooking, cleaning, marketing, and running our business. We were often exhausted long before night came.

We soon devised many ingenious ways to do things that we had previously asked someone else to do for us. It often took both of us to do a comparatively simple task that would involve holding or reaching for something.

We were delighted with our many wonderful wedding gifts. We had received a table and chair set, a desk and lamps, and we bought a living room set, kitchen stove and bedroom set. Of course, we didn't need seven rooms to live in; so two rooms in the back of our home became our workshops. Here we built shelves and tables for fly materials, storage, and typing space. We soon decided we needed more business space, so we took two more rooms. Our next biggest need was for a car. The war was still with us, and cars and gas were hard to obtain. Our local dealer got us a good used car that I was very proud of, although I couldn't drive it by myself. But we knew several people who would go with us to drive, if we could arrange a time with them.

Those first weeks we went to our local restaurant regularly every Friday evening for a steak dinner. It was a special occasion for us after working all week, and we looked forward to it.

We made several trips to Seaside on the Pacific coast so we could enjoy the mile-long cement promenade along the sandy beach. One day, while looking out over the ocean, we saw three whales spouting. We had never seen such a sight. We watched and watched. No one else seemed aware of the whales, until Bea and I pointed them out to the people next to us. It seemed that within minutes the whole prom was full of people watching.

Seaside also offered us our first chance to enjoy fishing together. There are several bridges across the Necanicum River within a few minutes of the promenade. Here we could go in our chairs by ourselves.

It wasn't very long before automobile hand controls became available for paraplegics and by that time we were able to buy a new car and have it equipped so I could drive it my-self. Able-bodied people will never know what it means for a handicapped person to be able to drive by himself. No more would we be dependent on others for transportation. Now we could decide where we wanted to go and just load our chairs and be on the road. It was a great feeling!

Driving a car brought us many experiences. Bea and I were still working with handicapped people in Portland. In fact, I was the national president of the Chin-Up Club at the time and was to be the speaker at a special banquet. Just south of Silverton, a rear tire on our Oldsmobile blew out and there we were. The only thing for me to do was to try to change it myself. I unloaded my chair on the gravel siding and finally got the car jacked up. Things were going pretty well and I thought, "Boy, this is going to be a cinch."

I got the wheel off and got the spare from the back easily enough. But whenever I lifted that heavy tire in front of my chair to put it on the car, my chair would tip forward and I would have to start all over again. Every time I would look up at Bea in the car, she would have her face turned away from me; but I couldn't help hearing her snicker. Finally I decided how I could get enough leverage to keep from tipping forward, and after that, everything went along as it should. When I was back in the car and we were safely on our way to Portland again, Bea laughed and laughed at how funny I had looked. We arrived just minutes before the banquet and by then it was funny to me too. But I never let that happen again. After that I let my motorclub do the work!

Bea and I met lots of interesting people during those first few years. Opal and Bill Judd, who were also both in wheelchairs, had met and married, and they lived in Milwaukie, near Portland. Our relationship with them has given us many happy memories, for both Opal and Bill know the Lord Jesus. We always felt spiritually renewed after spending time with them. Often our discussions about handicappers and our good Christian fellowship lasted until two A.M., after which Bea and I would have sixty miles to drive home and then have our shop open by eight A.M. as usual. But we treasured these experiences.

Bill and Opal are just one couple among hundreds of handicapped people we have known. I would like to mention many more of them but that is beyond the scope of this book.

During these years, Bea and I continued to work with young people at church. We taught church school classes, helped arrange entertainments, and worked in every way we could to further the Lord's work.

I remember particularly well a high school group I taught. We started with only a few in our class. As time went on, we tried to impress on our members their responsibility for witnessing of Christ to their unsaved friends. They began a practice of each one's being responsible for the attendance of another. Then their witnessing began to mean something to their friends and it began to bring many spiritual changes into their own lives. By the following year we were teaching twice as many young people.

One member of our class became ill, and her sister called to ask our group to hold a special prayer session for her. The girl's condition was grave and she was sinking. We called our group, held a prayer session, and found that our Lord could certainly send an answer. The girl's condition started to change from the hour we had met to ask God to undertake for her. Many young people became Christians as a result of these times and began to mature in their faith.

Years later, one girl wrote a letter telling us how she had held fast in her faith and had married, but had chosen subsequently to put her family before the Lord. Then she began to realize how much she needed her faith to help her raise her children as Christians. She told us she asked the Lord to forgive her, and then she began working actively in her church again. Now she is the mother of five, and all have given their hearts to the Christ whom the mother has so faithfully presented to them.

8

Business Ventures

As the days went by, we were constantly working at our manufacturing business. We also supplied special and regular flies to our local fishermen. We found an increasing number of people continually coming to our home to inquire if we had the regular supplies for every fishing trip.

One would ask, "Fred, will you get me a good fly rod and the right line to use it with?" Others inquired about trout baskets, sinkers, snelled hooks, nets, steelhead equipment, and even guns and ammunition. It seemed as if every time we talked to someone he wanted us to get some additional equipment for him.

There certainly was a need for a retail sporting goods store in Stayton. We talked the situation over and decided to ask several people who were more experienced in retailing to give us their opinions, and opinions we got!

"You can't take care of such a business!"

"What do you know about a retail outlet?"

"Are you educationally equipped to run a store?"

"You would always have to have a physically able person at the store to help you."

Over and over the theme recurred: "You can't run such a business from a wheelchair!"

I am just a simple person and I believed God had helped me all my life when I depended upon Him. I needed only to take Him at His word. It seemed to me that He was still answering my prayer. Opportunities were always there and if I didn't put effort to these opportunities, then I was the one not carrying my share in this partnership with God. So Bea and I decided we would stay with a motto that long had been in my shop and mind. It reads:

> "Somebody said it couldn't be done;
> But I with a chuckle replied
> That maybe it couldn't but I'd
>   not be the one
> To say so until I had tried.
>
> "So I buckled right in

With a bit of a grin on my face.
If I worried, I hid it.

"I started to sing as
I tackled the thing
That couldn't be done —
And I did it!"

(Author unknown)

So we decided to start our business with only a small amount of supplies and grow as the demand became known.

We were well acquainted with several sporting goods jobbing houses in Portland which we ourselves had supplied with flies. They had been buying from us and now we would become their customers. This was a great advantage for us, for they knew their brands and could really advise us on how we should stock our small store.

We actually thought it would take all season to sell our first stock order, but when the news got around that we had fishing supplies, we were back in Portland within two weeks, buying more. The season went along and we kept buying and selling each order even more quickly than we could anticipate. This was our start. One thing we were sure of was that we would need more space before another season came around. This could only be managed by a new building, so we contracted with a builder for an addition to the front of our house. It was to be attached so that we could also use four rooms of the house in the retail business. We were still manufacturing fishing flies, so we bought a building right across the street to house that business.

When spring rolled around, we were ready. We officially announced the opening of Camp's Sporting Goods, with a stock of fishing tackle, bicycles with service and parts, wheel goods, guns and ammunition.

Our first advertisement included mention of our repairing service; when this news got out, I really did start to work. I had never owned a bicycle, and I soon found out just how many parts each one had. I worked long and hard those first weeks to train myself by diagrams from each company to take every model apart and put it together correctly. I will never forget the first two-speed brake I encountered. I worked almost all night on that one and still wasn't satisfied. Eventually it seemed that all I needed was to really understand what the diagram meant. Finally this became clear to me after hours of repairing time and more patience than I ever thought I possessed.

Every time we felt we had learned all about the lines we handled, we would add a new one to the store. A salesman from a reputable company came to see us about toys and hobbies. He made us an offer: we would invest $500 in toys in June, and if we hadn't sold them by Christmas or before, he would take all remaining stock out of the store. We just couldn't lose on such an arrangement, so we let him decide what we should carry in stock. We were amazed to find we turned that first order of toys and hobbies over several times before the year's end. So we were in the toy business.

Bea enjoyed this probably far more than I did. She became the toy salesgirl. She sold many, many dolls as well as cars and airplanes. When a new shipment came in, she had a busy time marking, stocking shelves, and restyling the hair of every doll. It is surprising how this makes dolls more attractive and easier to sell.

We found a special value in handling several lines of franchised merchandise, including Schwinn bikes, Browning and Weatherby guns, Bausch and Lomb scopes, Johnson motors, Spalding and McGregor athletic goods and Bear archery supplies.

Our shop was full. We built another addition at the side which became our new repair shop. Then came the opportunity to take a new line — General Paint. This could be arranged on the same basis as the toy line. It also proved a financially successful venture.

Our business grew and we could see that we would have to hire help. We were working twelve to fourteen hours a day and we knew that we could not continue that. This was hard work, but it was not all drudgery. We enjoyed people of all ages. A little tot with a desire for a doll or a toy gun would leave with such a happy face when we had just the one wanted. A small boy who might want a new wagon or the wheels fixed on his old wagon was a delight to us. To that boy his coming to us was as important as the man who needed his fishing rod repaired. Couples who came in to do their Christmas shopping frequently ended up finding nearly all their gifts at our store. Then they left them to be wrapped so they could pick them up on Christmas Eve.

Many a newspaper boy depended on me to have his bicycle ready for the next morning's delivery, even if it had broken down at eight o'clock the night before. We enjoyed the fishermen, and many times I got up at two in the morning to write a license and supply equipment, so they could be on the lake by sunrise.

One day a man from the state vocational rehabilitation office came into the store. He wanted us to consider training other handicapped persons in our type of business. We could offer fly-tying, rod and reel repairing, gun reloading, bicycle repair, and small motor repair, along with a general education in operating a sporting goods store. We had never even considered this before. He had several interested handicapped men and felt that no one would be as efficient in training them as someone who knew exactly what problems they would have to face. This was a new venture for us and we were richly blessed in our association with these men during the following months. Just the fact that both Bea and I were in wheelchairs provided them the incentive to try things they would not have attempted under another type of supervision.

While we were in the store, I also learned to enjoy many sports I had never tried before, like fishing trips to mountain lakes with customer friends. I bagged nine deer on hunting trips. On each trip I found I would get to know a customer better as a friend, and I came to admire many of my regular customers for themselves alone.

Archery had come into its own in our town, and I joined the archery club. I found it was possible to maintain a better than average score even from a wheelchair.

Stayton has two creeks running through it,

and often I got up at five A.M. to go fishing, just wheeling from bridge to bridge and fishing from each one. When I couldn't leave the store during business hours on opening day of fishing, I would start early and be home with a limit of trout in time to go to work. I also landed several steelhead early in the morning. I remember one especially, because I caught it on my birthday on a four-pound test line. I played it for over an hour before the first fellow came along who could lift it from the water for me. This really made my birthday!

For about ten years, Bea and I operated both Camps Sporting Goods and our wholesale fly business. We worked early and late. It seemed each night was just not long enough for us to recuperate, and each morning found us hardly able to start again. After considerable discussion, we decided to sell the sporting goods store and put all our time into the fly business. We anticipated some difficulty in finding a buyer, as we knew much of our business had grown from personal contacts with our customers. Customers we had served only as fishermen soon bought gifts, toys and hobbies for themselves and their children. The lad who got his first tricycle from us got his Christmas toys from us, then his BB guns and fishing poles. As he grew he came to us for his archery goods, athletic equipment, and bicycle repairs. In ten years we had almost made a new cycle of customers. We found ourselves watching the development of many youngsters, for each one was extra special to us. We also came to the conclusion that boys who showed interest in sports and hobbies didn't cause parents much anxiety as teen-agers.

We never did advertise the store for sale, but in December I talked to several people who showed a special interest. In January the store was sold, and by March we were out of the retail business.

9

Julie Joins the Family

Now that we were free of the retail business, we started making plans for the fly season that would soon be in full swing. We decided to take several trips through the selling area and make personal contacts in order to enlarge our sales. Bea had not been feeling up to par, so we first had an appointment with our doctor for a complete physical.

After a few questions and tests, we were delighted to learn that we were to become parents. For ten years we had wanted to have a child of our own, but it seemed to be almost unheard of for two paraplegics to bring a child into the world. We had made contacts to see if one could be adopted, but always we got the same answer. Two handicapped people just don't meet the qualifications demanded of good prospective parents.

Now, more new plans had to be made. Our doctor said Bea must stay at home; there was to be no traveling for her. He didn't feel that she could do much work until after the baby was born. Our baby was to arrive about mid-September, so our idea of increasing our fly sales would have to wait. Under the circumstances I felt that I did not want to be away from the house very much either.

Those were trying months for Bea. She tired easily, and just the fact that she could not use her lower body caused her much discomfort and inconvenience. She took it as easy as possible and each day brought us closer to the time. Day by day, God gave her strength to face the next.

Like all prospective parents everywhere, we talked endlessly about names for both boys and girls. Finally we picked a name and from then on called our unborn child "Johnny." We really had no reason for deciding on a boy's name, but it just seemed natural because Bea's dad is named John. Naturally, we knew that either a boy or a girl would bring us great happiness.

We were looking forward to our baby's being born September 20, but on September first Bea suddenly became ill and her doctor advised immediate hospitalization. She had become dehydrated from constant nausea and required a nurse's care and intravenous feedings. She spent ten days on constant IV and then our doctor decided that the baby's time was due. Bea spent three days and nights in the labor room. Our doctor was wonderful. He practically lived at that hospital. After he had exhausted every means to bring the baby into the world naturally, he decided that the birth would have to be by Caesarean section.

I will never forget when Dr. Andersen told me, "Fred, you have been here at the hospital constantly, and I want you to go home and get some rest. We may save Bea but I can't be sure about the baby."

Here I was, an expectant father, not able to walk the floor to let off steam. My nerves were really in an uproar.

I drove home feeling as if I had the weight of the whole world on my shoulders. I couldn't conceive of life without Bea and didn't know how either of us could accept the loss of this baby we had already grown to love and consider an essential part of our lives.

It comes to my mind so clearly even now. I went into our kitchen, which had two large windows, and sat there looking up at the sky.

I said, "Lord, I don't know the answers, but I'm going to leave it all in Your hands.

You know what is best. Give Dr. Andersen wisdom and guide his every move, so that it all will be in Your will. You know what is best for all of us."

At that very moment it seemed that the load was lifted from me and my anxiety was gone. I had learned that the Creator of all was in command and I was willing to follow whatever He willed for us. I was at peace. I know now that whenever I ask God for something I had better mean it, for when He hears our plea, He will respond. The old song which says, "Take your burden to the Lord and leave it there," had been proven to me again.

Bea went into surgery about 1:30 that afternoon. I waited with Bea's mother and dad in the waiting room. In just a short time Dr. Meyn, who had assisted Dr. Andersen and Dr. Betzer, came from the surgery with my small daughter.

He showed her to me and said, "Fred, here's your new little one." Then he went into the nursery with her.

Minutes passed, minutes which seemed like hours, and then more minutes. I expected to see Bea coming from surgery at any time, but she didn't come when I thought she should. Now I know that completing such an operation takes more time than the child's birth. I felt I just couldn't wait until I knew what answer God had given me regarding my wife. I am so human I think I anticipated every possible condition. Just when I thought I could wait no longer, there came Bea on the surgery cart, accompanied by Dr. Andersen. He assured me he felt that everything would be all right now.

Our daughter soon had a new name. It wouldn't be Johnny, as we had thought. When Bea said, "Julie Ann" — well, there just didn't seem to be any question but that that name was just right for her. She became Julie Ann because my father whom I dearly loved was named Julius and my mother was Ann Margaret.

Our baby weighed six pounds, thirteen ounces at birth, and even as a tiny baby seemed never to be cross or easily disturbed. She slept soundly and grew rapidly. Her black hair and blue eyes just seemed to fit our Julie Ann and soon she was the one who drew all eyes. She was the little one who put such trust in me and in men in general. She refused to be held or fussed over by her aunties, but her uncles were really fine, to her way of thinking.

You just can't realize how much we loved that small daughter of ours. It seemed as though all life was new each time she discovered something or showed some new development in personality. She never seemed to be too much trouble for us. We knew we were extremely fortunate. She was a well child and her sleeping and eating habits were easily formed. We never knew what it was to have a sick child or a cross one. She seemed always to be on the positive side of life.

All too soon she was no longer a baby but a tiny girl, ready to do whatever we planned for her to have part in. We took her with us to church and on outings. When she was ten months old, she made her first fishing trip with us to a mountain lake at the summit of the Cascades. She had her own bed and comforts and proved to be a good trouper. After that we took her quite regularly. She enjoyed picnics; she loved to go riding in the country where we often saw squirrels, pheasants, quail, and occasionally owls and deer. We found many things to do which kept us all happy, and the fact that Bea and I were in wheelchairs never seemed to keep us from thoroughly enjoying ourselves. As Julie grew, we often took her fishing and hunting. By the time she was four, she had caught her first fish and retrieved game. She was so proud to think she could go and get a pheasant or a quail. Bea and I tried to do all we could with her without engaging any other help. We knew that later she would remember how we were a family together.

After she was older, I often took her to town and we would go to the bakery for a doughnut and coffee or Coke. She was always ready and one of her first inquiries would be, "Dad, are we going to stop for a doughnut?"

Julie would entertain herself at one end of our fly shop. She had a spring-horse that she called Black Prince. Many hours were spent keeping old Black Prince on the gallop. And she was a very imaginative child. She could spend an afternoon with plastic cowboys and Indians, animals and rocks and logs, making a real layout on the living room floor. She would have to place everything just right before she was pleased with her work. Then she would come to us and want us to hurry and see it before all the Indians and cowboys got away.

Some of my most wonderful memories of Julie are of the mornings at the breakfast table when she was still a small child. I would get her up and when I let the side of her crib down she would crawl over into my lap, look up to me with a big smile, kiss me good morning, and out to breakfast we would go. Before she ate, she always had to get down and go to see Bea who somehow had acquired the habit of having breakfast in bed.

After a few minutes with Bea we were ready to have our breakfast.

I always planned to have at least a half-hour at the table. Julie enjoyed stories, so every morning I would make up a story about Peter Rabbit or "A Little Boy in a Yellow Raincoat." Each story had a moral or spiritual lesson which would become a part of her life. She loved these stories and I don't believe I could have read her books which would have fascinated her as much. As she grew older, we always had our devotions together. I typed out many small verses from the Bible. We would lay them down in front of us in a stack and Julie would take one and see if she could remember it by the reference to chapter and verse. Then she would see if I could. She learned many verses this way.

Bea and I planned, of course, to bring our child up to know the Lord. We wanted her to realize what it really meant to be a Christian and to give Him first place in her life. We took her to church regularly and when she was just a toddler she began attending Sunday school. To her, Sunday was meant for Sunday school and church and then other pleasant activities.

10

Family Fun on Wheels

Until Julie was four we operated our fly business. Every day seemed to keep us busy. Bea, of course, needed time for the home and Julie, and she often didn't get to work with me except when Julie had her naps. During these hours Bea helped with finishing and shipping flies.

I had missed the retail sporting goods business and was interested in getting into it again. About this time we learned that the man who purchased the store from us was also planning a change and wanted to go into the newspaper business, for which he was very adequately trained. After some negotiations, we again became the owners and operators of Camp's Sporting Goods.

It didn't take us long to get back into the

swing of the store and I thoroughly enjoyed both our old customers and our new ones. Bea helped in the store and Julie was often the tiny "sales person" who answered questions from people who said, "I have a little girl about your age, honey. What toys do you like?"

Julie was easy to have around and soon became known to all those customers who were our old friends. Somehow she realized store toys did not belong to her and she left them alone. Her interests centered in the yard, in older children, and in thinking about going to kindergarten and first grade.

Those were the years of family fun — picnics, drives, trips to the ocean and to the mountains. Confinement to our wheelchairs didn't stop us from enjoying the vast amount of outdoor activity that was possible for us. Bea and I wanted Julie to be an outgoing and open person.

Now I realize that our eagerness to help Julie develop caused us to plan far more things than most parents do. We went hunting. We took the car and gun and drove out to the farms. Most of them were owned by our customers and friends and they were most hospitable. Of course we hunted from the car but our state allows handicapped persons to do this if they obey state laws and do not shoot across a roadway. We drove miles, stopping to see cattle grazing or a band of sheep which had just lambed or some horses or pigs or just robins, doves, or migrating goldfinch. We didn't plan to kill a lot of game, but we did get our share of pheasants and quail.

One day we had seen several pheasants, but all seemed to be in a place where a four-year-old would have trouble retrieving them, so we passed these up. Finally we spotted a big pheasant rooster just inside a fence. I asked Julie if she thought she could get through the fence, and she was sure she could. She was ready.

Now to make my shot good. I fired and the rooster toppled over. Out of the car Julie went, down on her tummy and under the barbed wire and over to get the rooster. She was acting as though she had the whole world in her hand. She pulled the rooster back to the fence and held it as though it might vanish at any time. In the meantime rain started coming down. Somehow in the process she had found a much harder place to climb back through, but down on her tummy she went. I laughed as the barbed wire caught the seat of her pants. She just couldn't get away, until with a big pull that left shreds of cloth dangling from the wire, she got loose and returned to the car triumphantly.

"I think I tore my pants," she said, "but I got the pheasant!" She later retrieved many others on unfenced land, but this one was special to her and to me.

Another time we were out hunting for quail. I spotted a few in a corn patch. I didn't know how many there were. Just about the same time I saw them, Julie saw them too. She waited for me to shoot and out she went. She came back with three but I knew I had hit more than that. After a search she rounded up ten in all — my whole limit for the day. She thought I was pretty great, bagging my limit, all with one shot!

Our trips took us all around Oregon. We visited the Reindeer Ranch and Peterson's Rock Gardens near Bend. Her enjoyment of the Rock Gardens meant the beginning of a rock collection which she has continued into her teen years.

We traveled Century Drive and the high lakes regions. She fished Elk, Ease, Blue, Suttle, Crescent Lakes and many more. Julie was not at all squirmy about putting a worm on a hook. Often at home she helped me count out worms for store customers. She also became interested in insects and butterflies and moths and developed quite extensive collections of all of these.

Other trips took us down the Columbia

Basin, through the Crater Lake area, down the Rogue and Umpqua Rivers, through the redwoods, and up and down the Oregon beaches. We also made several trips in Washington state. Julie loved to travel and she never hesitated to visit aquariums, museums, fishing docks, or any tourist attraction. She was always ready to go; and even when we encountered barriers for wheelchairs, she would visit places of interest by herself. We knew she would follow our instructions, and she would only be gone so long before she came back. She loved Seaside on the coast with its wide cement promenade. We would rent a child's bike for her and we would all three go from one end to the other — Bea in her chair and I in mine and Julie way out in front on her bike.

Even yet Julie loves to fish with her grandfather Nightingale. It's always a race and a bet as to who will catch the first and largest fish. She thinks her grandfather is the world's best fishing companion.

As we traveled and saw spectacular views of mountains, deep valleys, high cliffs, or the rolling river, we would talk of how God must have had just such people as us in mind when He planned such beautiful places for our enjoyment.

We had the opportunity to see the Santiam

Canyon many times. One summer, when the small community church in Idanha, east of Stayton, was without a pastor for awhile, I was asked to fill the pulpit. Idanha Community Church is situated in a small clearing in a beautiful place across the North Santiam River. Through the door one sees snow-covered Mount Jefferson, looking so near you could reach out and touch it. Each Sunday Bea and Julie would start up the canyon with me to travel the forty miles to the church. It was a wonderful experience for me. How grateful I was to be given opportunity to witness to these people, to feel even more of God's presence in my life, and to tell others of His wonderful Word!

11

Trips to Remember

My doctor had always told me that I should not work such long hours but should take more time to relax and enjoy life more. I ignored his advice for a long time; but finally, as I was getting ready to go to bed one night about 12:30, I decided he was right.

I had worked all day and all evening, and I decided to bathe before retiring. Everything had been going along fine; but as I used my arms to pull my weight from the tub, one hand slipped and down I went. With extreme effort I finally managed to pull myself out of the tub and into my chair. Bea was already asleep, so I made my way painfully into bed. But within just a few minutes, I simply could not move. I called Dr. Andersen and he came immediately. The doors were locked but the bedroom window was open, so he jumped the picket fence and came in that way. After examining my shoulder, he felt I should have X-rays at the hospital. He called the ambulance, helped me dress, and opened the doors when the ambulance arrived. He insisted that Bea stay in bed, saying he would call her to give her details. We were all relieved to find that my shoulder was not broken, but the muscles were severely pulled. I spent the next week in the hospital and there decided those trips to the lake would be my next undertaking. Maybe I did need more relaxation!

I recall with much pleasure a trip to East Lake, formed in an old volcano forty miles from Bend, Oregon. It is a beautiful lake, at high elevation. I made the trip with four friends, but it was cold — so cold I wrapped myself in a sleeping bag during the day, but even then I nearly froze as we sat in the boat on the lake. My impaired circulation made it impossible for me to keep warm. But for honest-to-goodness fishing I never enjoyed anything so much before. I caught fish when no one else could. I had discovered the feeding level of those trout and whenever I got to that depth, I had a trout on. I caught my limit in a short time and helped my friends who were not having any luck at all. We all came home with a limit, but it took me almost four days to thaw out!

One trip to Triangle Lake was another highlight of my fishing. Both Bea and I had fished Triangle, and I had been there several times with different people. This time we were with Art and Fern, a couple whom Bea and I especially enjoyed.

Triangle Lake lies in the coast range. It is a pretty lake, sheltered from the wind. Almost every morning a fog lies over the clear water, and it is so quiet you can actually hear the fish jump. One interesting thing about the lake is that fish are reported to jump higher out of the water here than in any other lake in the world. Ripley himself said so in his "Believe It or Not" column. Just as the sun starts to come up over the lake, the water becomes as smooth as a mirror; and when the fish start jumping, it is as if they spiral from way down in the depths of the lake. They have actually jumped all around us and we have often wondered if one might not land in our boat.

When you are out on the lake, it is the most natural thing in the world to look up at the wonders of nature and think with David of old in Psalm 8:3 and 4: "When I consider thy heavens, the work of thy fingers, the moon and the stars, which thou hast ordained; what is man, that thou art mindful of him?"

Handicapped people miss much pleasure by

not taking advantage of boat fishing. This is one sport where we can really be on a par with any other fisherman. All you need is hands to hold the rod and vigor enough to reel in the fish. I know there are places where the handicapped cannot go; but if you have someone to help you into a boat, you really can enjoy fishing.

As we boated across Triangle this particular day, we were only thinking about getting to the other side to fish. We were passing some old pilings, and just for fun I cast a white flatfish next to the piling. I actually thought I snagged up and asked my friend to stop the boat. To my surprise the line became alive! I had a big bass on. I knew I must be very careful and take it easy as I had only a light line. We were out in the open where I had plenty of room, and I gradually worked him up to the boat. He was the largest bass I had ever caught — four pounds, to the ounce.

One day when Bea and I were out in the boat with our friends, we found the fishing to be terrific. We caught all we needed or even wanted, but the fish continued to strike. As we rowed along, it seemed that each cast or so gave us another bass on flies. So we started to catch them and turn them loose. It was a hot day and Bea and Fern were really ready to go in, but Art and I just couldn't quit with so much fun to be had. I wouldn't have blamed the girls if they had dumped us in the lake.

We did not usually use our Sundays for fishing, but it was the only day Art and Fern could go with us. An attractive thing about Triangle Lake was that the small church on the lakeshore sent its Sunday services over the lake by loudspeaker. I made sure we were well within hearing distance. Neither of our friends was accustomed to attending church, so the service stimulated many questions and some good discussion. Today Art and Fern both know the Lord and both are active in their church. Now we talk about those days and declare, "God works in mysterious ways His wonders to perform."

Davis Lake is another place which gives me pleasant memories. This was the first lake we ever took Julie to, although she was too young to remember it later. One Indian summer day, two of my fisherman friends and I drove up Willamette Pass to Davis Lake, right on the Cascade Summit. It was breathtakingly beautiful. It was as if all nature was dressed in its finest colors; the dogwood, the vine maple and all the trees looked just like the rainbow itself.

We arrived at the lake early and no one

else was there. It was the last day of fishing on this lake and only deer romped around the deserted campgrounds. As we launched our boat and pushed off, it was very cold. In fact, it was so cold the ice formed in my line guides as we fished. As the sun came up, it warmed the air and our day of fishing began. At first we couldn't get a single strike, so we decided to head for the lava rocks across the lake and fish there.

Here we cast into the lava rocks on the shore and let the fly fall back into the water. Then we slowly retrieved it. The first one we caught was a three-pound rainbow and he gave us a battle. He was the smallest one we got all day — the others weighed as much as four pounds. One strike hit Wilbur's line so hard he lost all his line and fly. We would surely have enjoyed seeing that lunker again, but we never did. The fish were wary. We could actually see a trout take the fly; but if we didn't set the hook immediately, he would literally spit it out.

Davis Lake is noted for a period of rough water each day, but as we were fishing in a cove sheltered from the wind, we forgot all about time. We started home as soon as we noticed the breaks in the water, but home was five miles away. On the way our boat was blown toward some mud flats, and it took us a long time to work away from them and back to the landing. In spite of that problem it was really a day of good fishing that Wilbur, Ed, and I will long remember.

Suttle Lake, also in the Cascades, is one we fished many times. One time we went with Delbert, his wife Billie, and their two children. Billie is a remarkable person. Although she is not sighted, she loves out-of-door life and recreation. A list of her achievements is overwhelming. She is efficient in all that she does. She is an excellent mother, taking care of all her family's needs. She is a seamstress and makes mother and daughter dresses so expertly that you would think they were professionally tailored. She is a fine cook and baker. She enjoys books in Braille, and loves music and plays. She has a wonderful helper in her husband who has learned through the years to talk in a very picturesque language to her. Her children shared their world with her, and we were always amazed when her boy would come running after catching a frog or whatever it might be. He would say, "Hey, Mom, come and see," as he placed her hand over his newfound treasure and described it beautifully for her. It was always a delight for Bea and me to go places with them.

Detroit Reservoir in the Santiam Canyon was close to us and was one of the lakes I fished regularly. The access for a wheelchair is good at the resorts in early season and later from Mongold Landing. I have found the resort owners very cooperative and willing to help with both boat and motor, but I usually took only my motor and rented their boats. The scenery is beautiful there. You can fish along the cliffs or near Piney Island, from which you can see a waterfall high up in the mountains coming out of another lake. This lake and waterfall are accessible only by foot. You really appreciate God's creation from such scenic wonders.

Although I have fished there often and taken many limits of fish, I shall long remember the day Willis and I had been fishing. It was a windy day, but I had my life jacket on as I always do when in a boat. I really wasn't worried until white caps began to appear and occasionally our boat would take water. Then I was ready to go in. I still was not worried, as I had my jacket on. But after we docked the boat and were unloading, I found to my surprise that the anchor rope was caught around my life jacket belt. I had been tied to the anchor and would have gone right down to the bottom with it, if we had capsized. I was rather weak after we got out of the boat and began to realize how much danger we really had been in.

When I had been working hard and wanted to get away, I would often go up to Detroit by myself, get into a boat and row out from the dock into a cove about twelve feet deep. It was clear enough to see the bottom. I would set up my tackle and watch for fish. This particular day I could see an old rainbow below the boat. I would toss an egg in the water and he would take it. Let me put an egg out with a hook in it and that was the end of the action. I got so engrossed that I played with him for about two hours. Finally I left my bait on the bottom, on the line, and then fed him one egg after another. As each fell to the bottom, he would go closer and closer to my setup. Finally he got careless, and wham! He got my bait. It was the only fish I got that day, but I never caught one that I had more fun with. I really considered turning him loose, but I knew how much Bea and Julie loved trout. So home he went with me.

I had a delightful trip drifting the Deschutes River in Central Oregon with a couple of friends. We got a nice limit of fish, but I was even more pleased to see so many animals in their natural habitat.

Several times I drifted the Santiam River down from Stayton to Green's Bridge. There are many places along this area that are inaccessible except by boat. Sometimes we would spin-fish and sometimes fly-fish. It is a good area and a very beautiful one.

We became acquainted with a family who had never been fishing; since it was near the start of school, we began to talk about taking one trip with them before September first. So we started out to Siltcoos Lake below Florence, Oregon, on the coast. It is a large lake having some forty miles of shoreline and the reputation of being a place to catch all the yellow perch, blue gill, and catfish you want. I really enjoy yellow perch, often preferring it to trout.

Bea and I, with fifteen more people, caught 300 perch and catfish during our three-day stay. It was a ball! We ate fish for dinner, fish for lunch, and fish for breakfast. Bea says she had never cleaned so many fish in her life. The weather was beautiful, with no wind or clouds. Everyone caught fish and sometimes two at a time. We rented three fishing cabins all in one row, so of course no one got any sleep. All were busy with wolf calls, midnight visits, and pranks, but all in just good fun! It was a highlight of our lives.

These are but a few of our trips. I honestly can say this: give me a boat, a rod, and a boat seat and I will forget I cannot walk or use my legs. These trips have provided wonderful fun and recreation for our "family on wheels."

12

Another Home

For many years it had been my desire to give Bea a new home. She had always been such a faithful helper, working so diligently at my side. Julie was now a fourth grader and I had found my health more and more a thing to be considered. I had never recovered completely from the pulled shoulder, and bursitis had become one of my constant ailments. My hands also showed that the gout in my system was growing progressively worse, and at times I could hardly lift anything or use my fingers to any advantage. Besides this, I was suffering from one or two severe migraine headaches a week.

I knew that if we were ever to build a home, it would have to be soon. It was our desire to send Julie to a Christian school and the closest one was in Salem, Oregon. So we decided to examine some houses there to see if we could find one that would meet our needs. I also knew that I would have to sell my retail store again, and, as before, a few inquiries were all I needed to find a buyer.

We visited several real estate agents and looked at many houses, but we just didn't find one that we could really enjoy without spending a lot more to remodel it for our use. Finally we talked to a contractor and found he could build us one for even less than the prebuilts would cost, considering the remodeling expense.

So we began to work on house plans. We had talked for a number of years about what we wanted in a home, but now we were faced with actually putting it down on paper. There were so many things to consider. We wanted a house in which we could be independent of others' help. This meant no steps. It meant wide hallways, lower kitchen built-ins, larger windows above the sink, and other windows that we ourselves could open and close, a large patio, an oversized garage, cement sidewalks around the yards and house, electric-eye garage doors, a built-up fireplace to make it easy to clean and to make fires from our chairs, a legless breakfast bar, and large sliding doors to bedrooms and to our patio. Our built-ins were all to be made of natural golden birch, and each shelf in our lower built-ins was to pull out so that a minimum amount of bending would be necessary to get articles from remote corners. Our bathrooms were designed to give accommodations to a wheelchair and still appear no different from other bathrooms. We wanted radiant electric heat, a dishwasher, a garbage disposal, a built-in oven and range, a large refrigerator, an extra large deep freeze, a washer, a dryer, and birchwood accordian doors on the upper built-ins and on the sewing room doors off the utility room.

Finally we got our plans drawn and the building started in southeast Salem on one-fourth acre of land. Bea had always enjoyed gardening and this would offer her plenty of room inside a redwood backyard fence and around the house area to grow plants and shrubs to her heart's content.

In six months, on April first, we moved into our "dream house" and Julie started to a new school. A new venture was in store for all of us. We spent an exciting spring and summer, putting in lawns and shrubs and planting flowers. Before fall came, we were all settled down. It was really all we had expected of a new home in a quiet, friendly neighborhood; for life now was a big change from the Stayton home and store and busy road which was constantly filled with log trucks, farm equipment, and cars. At first we couldn't decide why our new home seemed so quiet, but we had only to drive back to Stayton to understand.

We had a delightful housewarming to which our families came from Portland, Eugene and, of course, Stayton. This officially opened our new home.

Bea has always enjoyed cooking and entertaining, and she now has the conveniences and space to have family and friends in for dinners and special occasions. Now enough room was available to serve a number of people in other than buffet style. In the winter we have dinners and in the summer, patio cookouts. It has been a part of our lives we have really enjoyed.

A popular annual event is the Fourth of July picnic held "at the Camps" for members of the Chin-Up Club, some of our dearest friends. Each year we have hosted a group of about fifty. Of course, our house does not accommodate that many, but we convert the garage to a large dining room, complete with tables, benches, and decorations, for we have lots of good food. Our back yard becomes a play yard, for many of our friends who have no other opportunity to participate in games become athletes that day. We play croquet, archery, lawn darts, catch, checkers and whatever anyone might like to do.

These are all things that people in wheelchairs can do. Even people who aren't able to use their arms seem to enjoy the time they spend here on the Fourth, just going around the cement walks and viewing Bea's flowers. It's always a busy day. Friendships are cemented and people who have never before opened their lives to enjoy other people become part of the group on such a day.

Julie is always a big help for this occasion. She has an understanding of handicapped people that not many realize, because our friends are also her friends. To her a wheelchair is just a means of conveyance, not something that sets one person apart.

About 10 P.M. when the last guests have departed, Bea usually finds out how tired she is; nevertheless, each year we always come to the same conclusion when we talk together that it really *is* worth the effort to have these friends in.

I mentioned Bea's garden. It has been a delight to her. When I miss her from the house, all I need do is look out the patio door to find her. I stay completely out of it as far as gardening is concerned. I do enjoy each flower and shrub, but I know very little about their growing habits. We have many flowers — azaleas, rhododendrons, daphne, roses, quince, mock orange, calla lilies as well as tiger, trumpet and pink lady lilies. We have crocus, tulips, dutch and bearded iris, peonies, and many, many more. Bea has 400 feet of four-foot-wide border. Julie and I take care of the lawn and lawn cutting — an easy item for me, for I purchased a riding lawn mower and equipped it with hand controls so I can also join in the back yard fun.

Our sidewalks have provided fun for the neighborhood children. Sometimes we have a dozen of them with their bicycles, playing at street patrolling. We enjoy these days and they seem to understand that our grass and flowers are not to be disturbed. They are very good about minding when they infrequently need correction.

We have lived in our Salem home seven years. Our daughter, now almost grown, has had the privilege of attending Salem Academy, a Christian junior and senior high school where she is an upper classman. We have been happy about this education for her, as we have been able to watch her development into Christian womanhood.

We have often talked about what might have been done differently in building our home and have always seemed to come to the conclusion that there aren't any major things we would change if we were to build another. We surely are grateful to God for our home and for this happy time in our lives.

13

How to Help the Handicapped

Many people have asked me questions about handicapped people. How should they be treated? How can their family and friends be of most help to them? Through the years I have observed many things about rehabilitating handicapped people and have discovered why it seems so difficult for some, nearly impossible for others, and almost unnecessary for the rest.

First I should say that there are many, many kinds of handicapped people. Some are only slightly indisposed, some almost entirely helpless, and some seem never able to even consider their lives on the same level as their able-bodied friends and family.

Rehabilitation begins at the outset — from the very time the accident or disease results in disability; and its degree of success is generally determined by — surprisingly — the family. I have known families who make it almost impossible for their handicapped to be rehabilitated. Many are so filled with love and concern that they do not allow the handicapped ever to get out on his own. They are so anxious that everything be done for their loved one that they prevent him from rising to face the problems of this world. They don't do this knowingly, but the result is the same. It is essential for the handicapped to learn to manage all his own care. Even though it might be most difficult and awkward for him to do so, he should have this privilege. Until he accomplishes this, he cannot go ahead to work toward any livelihood or even to fill his time meaningfully. Some families are so overprotective that their handicapped member isn't even allowed to get a glass of water for himself. If this goes on for a number of years, one can readily understand how empty that person's life will become. He is not proud of himself; he feels he can do nothing; therefore, life becomes meaningless. He doesn't care about his appearance. His ideas are shallow. He wants only to crawl into a shell and hope that his existence on this earth will not be long.

Remember, the handicapped person has a

great responsibility for his own future. He must be able, whether with one person or a group, to have the public look beyond his handicap and see only the man. I have heard many people say, "Why, we don't even consider that you are in a wheelchair." Then I feel good. I feel I have become completely rehabilitated in that person's eyes. I have found that the less I say about myself the better. Then I am not being continually reminded of my disability.

It takes many heartbreaks and many times of heart mending to know that one will never be able to walk again. Often the "if only's" become uppermost in a handicapped person's mind. "If only I could" can be a devastating emotion one must constantly guard against.

"I am this way — and as I am today, I will be tomorrow and tomorrow and tomorrow" is a fact that must be realized and must be accepted. The permanently handicapped must not be encouraged to feel that his affliction is only a passing thing. This only tempts him to put off helping himself. Today must be important and its best use must be a motivation to bring about a better tomorrow.

Unfortunately, many handicapped people become rehabilitated only to a degree. They are not able to accept the weight of their whole disability. They wish to think they cannot go beyond the easiest part of recovery. They remain housebound. They never go beyond the house door because of the staring eyes of their neighbors. They forget how readily others adjust to unusual things.

A person will often say of some object of art or some neighborhood development, "I could never get used to having *that* around." But as days pass and he grows accustomed to it, the item loses in his eyes its unfavorable qualities. This is the way with a handicap. My wife and I have been in chairs for so long that I know, if by some miracle we should no longer need our wheels, we would have to make many new friendships. So many of our friends just wouldn't know us or feel that we were the same people. They know us and like us for what we *are,* not for the way we look or don't look. I have been in this chair since I was eighteen, more than forty years, and Bea since she was eighteen, more than thirty years. Needless to say, we manage all phases of our lives by ourselves and people admire us for it.

We often point out that we may not do things as quickly as some people do, but just give us time and we will do it. Many amusing things have happened on this account through the years. We have caused people many a chuckle as they see some of the unusual ways we have learned to live in this world.

I remember one time my brother and I were visiting some friends. We didn't intend to stay long when we arrived, but they insisted we come in for awhile. I had not taken my chair and so my brother just carried me into the house and put me down in an ordinary chair. We visited for some time, then something took everyone but me into the living room, leaving me alone in the kitchen. A friend of their family came in and then he too decided to go to the living room.

I said, "Why don't you carry me in there?" He seemed so strong and husky that I felt this would not be anything too difficult for him to do.

He looked at me rather strangely and then picked me up. Starting to laugh, he headed for the living room, having no idea I couldn't walk. He set me down on a chair; and when he later found out about my handicap, he could hardly believe it.

"I almost dropped you purposely," he said. "I was going to tell you to walk the rest of the way by yourself and not to be so lazy."

Another incident of this kind happened after Bea and I were married. We had gone with her sister's family to visit Bea's aunt and uncle. There wasn't room for chairs in the car, so we decided to have my brother-in-law just carry us in. We visited for awhile and then another couple came. We chatted for nearly an hour, and then my brother-in-law said, "I think we'd better go." He picked me up and carried me out to the car.

This couple did a double take and said, "What is this? Some kind of game?"

Then he returned for Bea, picked her up and out they went too. The other guests were completely amazed — little had they realized neither of us could walk.

Bea and I have always made it a point to do all the usual things in public life, just as our able-bodied friends do. We have taken part in community affairs, church activities, and club activities. We have done all our own shopping, marketing, and banking. We have appeared on programs and taught classes. We have enjoyed sports and have helped with children's activities. We have worked and played as all people do.

Through the years we have encountered many obstacles. Public buildings and businesses often are off-limits to us due to steps and escalators. Public streets nearly all have the inconvenience of the step down from curbs, and often we are forced to cross streets in the middle of a block where the alley affords us an incline. It is a necessity to parallel park, as one cannot climb a curb when diagonally parked. On occasion we have wheeled for as much as three or four blocks down alleys to get to a business where we needed to go.

Frequently, we have much difficulty finding rest rooms to accommodate us and must go back home because of it. Restaurants never seem to have a rest room equipped to handle a wheelchair. I once went to a banquet for handicapped people from all over the state of Oregon and found no available restroom service for our people, many of whom had come several hundred miles to attend that affair.

Often people fail to realize how busy the handicapped can be. He may appear idle when talking to someone, but it takes him more time for his personal care; and if he is engaged in any type of business, he will have even less time. I remember one dear lady who wanted me to draw her the Little Abner characters. I had several days of work ahead of me, but I agreed to help her. When she returned, her comment was, "I just thought you might enjoy doing something for someone." Her work had taken me two days and I never go so much as a thank you. And I still had all my own work to do!

We have often been distressed by the thoughtlessness of clerks in retail stores. Some are excellent, but I can easily find one who seems to think all people in wheelchairs have loads of time. I have had many a clerk wait on a whole line of customers and then finally say, "Now, maybe I can help you."

I have also observed clerks who assume that a handicapped person is just naturally looking for the most inexpensive item there is to buy. They don't seem to realize that a handicapper as often as not has enough money to pay for a nice article.

Many people pay no attention to handicaps. Some are always ready to help and are so anxious that they do not stop to inquire how one wants to be helped. I have noticed this particularly when I get into our car. I know I must use my feet as leverage and that I must swing my body at the proper angle or I will land on the ground. I always appreciate help pulling in my chair, but often I must say, "No, I'll manage," to my would-be helper or I might find myself under the car instead of in it. When people simply ask *how* they can help, everything goes great.

My wife and I seem to be slated each year to spend some time in a hospital. We have made it a point to go to the same doctor for years and he fully realizes our capabilities and our conditions. He puts us in the same hospital each time and the nurses there are aware that we can take care of ourselves. Last year I went to a different hospital and found that nurses there handled people the same way whether they were handicapped or able-bodied. We had some difficulty until they recognized that I knew how my body reacted and they did not, because they were not accustomed to my needs. Then all went fine.

I have always found that a handicapped person who is idle and feels dejected generally feels his aches and pains are almost more than he can bear, because he has only that to think about. Before I was in business, I was sure that each pain was the forerunner of a condition much worse than I already had. I found that the busier I became, the less I had time to worry and to fret; consequently, the less my aches and pains bothered me. I found I had to be really ill before I would go to a doctor and not work. Just keeping busy relieves many aches and pains.

While in the retail business I was amused many times at the expressions on the faces of people who came in for the first time and found me in a wheelchair. They often asked how I managed and I assured them I had very little difficulty. About that time Bea would arrive, and they would be doubly amazed to find us both in chairs. Then to know we were the owners and operators of the store seemed to just bowl them over. But we found people accepted us in the same manner we accepted them. If we were always friendly, we found others the same way.

Always remember, a handicapper is a person, one exactly like you. He doesn't want pity or special treatment, or sympathy. In fact, he rebels within himself when he knows that you regard him as an "unfortunate." He wants to be like you, to be your friend, and your equal. He wants you to talk to him about all the things you would tell another person. He wants to be trusted.

So, remember, the best way to help the handicapped is to show him he is needed and respected in this world.

14

Between God and Man

People have told me that when the going was rough for them, they looked at Bea and me and began counting their blessings. We are happy the Lord can use us in this way and we thank Him for it.

Some handicapped people feel that their affliction is a punishment from God, and they say, "Why, oh, why did God do this to me?" But nothing could be farther from the truth. God may allow suffering, but He does it for a very real purpose.

David wrote in Psalm 119:67: "Before I was afflicted, I went astray." Sometimes the Lord must lay us down so we can look up. This may be the only way He can reach us, for He wants us to be with Him through all eternity. In order to get us to stop and face the real peril of our lost condition without knowing Christ as our Savior, He may be using an affliction, our handicap, to reach us.

It could be that God could not trust anyone else to suffer the way we do, that we are the only one who can take this trial and let Him use us to His glory. He may want our affliction to be a blessing that will help someone else over a rough path.

What most people do not realize is that the Lord places more value on our weakness than on our strength, because when we are strong we don't depend on Him the way we do when we are consciously weak. He wants us to rely on His resources and let Him show His glory forth through us.

Look at God's giants in the Bible. They were all weak men whose great acts occurred only because they counted on God's being with them and acting through them. In His ministry on earth Christ was concerned for the poor and the handicapped people in distress. He made the lame to walk, the deaf to hear, the blind to see. Today He is still concerned about you, whether you are in physical or spiritual need. No matter how much you might have to bear, no matter how much sorrow or pain you might have to suffer, He wants to give you strength and understanding and insight into His Word and His ways so that you will have a ministry of blessing to others.

As I close this book, may I get really personal? How handicapped are you? If you have no physical handicap, would you admit to having a spiritual handicap?

I have spent thirteen chapters telling, with my life as the example, that all is not lost when a person becomes partially or even fully handicapped. Some might say I have preached the message of self-help, of finding full rehabilitation by getting up and going and doing and seeing, telling, loving, and being; that by refusing to give in to the idea that this world has no place for me in my weakness, I have overcome the limitations of my condition.

True, I am as mobile as many. I have been able to freely enjoy hunting and fishing and other outdoor activities. I have succeeded in business. I have hosts of friends and have been able to be an encouragement to many other handicapped people through the Chin-Up Club. I have my own lovely family and my own happy home where supreme contentment reigns. And true, it has come to me because I have done two things: I've determined not to be a vegetable and I've gotten myself up and out and down the road of this life.

But there is another side to it. Self-help

was *not* all the answer, because the strange thing is that the most important part of life itself is just the opposite. I needed help that I couldn't give myself and I had to turn to God. And my condition is just a picture of the plight of everyone else the world over.

All mankind is helplessly handicapped when it comes to doing something to get into a right relationship to God. Self-help can do nothing to satisfy Him. Going, doing, seeing, telling, loving, and being are of no help in obtaining forgiveness of sins. It's "not by works of righteousness which we have done, but according to His mercy He saved us" (Titus 3:5). For, you see, we have all sinned. Not one of us is naturally righteous. We all want our own way and we know we don't always do what we ought. But God has said that the person who sins must die for his sins. God has standards of righteousness because He is holy. Sinfulness and holiness are mutually exclusive.

The thing is, God gives us an opportunity to accept a righteousness we cannot earn; and here we handicapped people have the jump on everybody else. We've actually known what it means to be completely helpless and have someone else do things for us. This is God's way. He knew we could not pay a penalty big enough to erase our sin. Therefore, He Himself paid the penalty.

In the person of the Lord Jesus Christ, God came into this world to live and to let everyone see that He was perfect God and perfect Man. Then He gave His life as a sacrifice, big enough to erase all our sins, big enough to pay the world-sized penalty to satisfy a holy God.

In the Old Testament a lamb was slain at regular intervals to remind people constantly that there was a way to acceptance with God. The offerer could do nothing but stand in the good of the sacrifice. Now God has accepted the sacrifice of the greater Lamb, the Lord Jesus. By repenting of our sins and accepting Christ's death as paying the penalty we would have had to pay ourselves, we stand in the good of that sacrifice and God accepts us.

He has done for us what we could never do for ourselves. We handicapped can see this so clearly because we've been helpless physically, and we can the more easily see how helpless we are spiritually. Each of us needs to repent of his own sins and ask God to save us from sin's penalty on the merit of the death of Christ Himself.

No handicapped person can find happiness or real contentment in this life until he knows Christ as his personal Savior. Then He will sustain the believer throughout all his days of affliction.

This has been my experience. Remember how I bargained with God on my own terms and got nowhere? Then I prayed on His terms and stood in the good of His righteousness and He added to my life all the blessings that had been my greatest desires — a business, a wife, a home and a family. I have experienced the sweet goodness of the Lord, and I have learned, in the words of Philippians 4:11, "in whatsoever state I am, therewith to be content."

This has been my experience. I pray it may be yours too, and that this may be for you — as each new day is for me —

The Beginning